AF408447

MOVERS MARKETING
A No B.S. Guide for Moving Companies to Win on Google and Maximize ROI

Amazon eBook: B0FQ5WBT6Q
Amazon Paperback ISBN: 9798265043627
eBook ISBN: 9798234009364
Paperback ISBN: 9798234009357

Cover design by Mike Zafiropoulos

ZafroCreative.com

Edited by Hilary Jastram

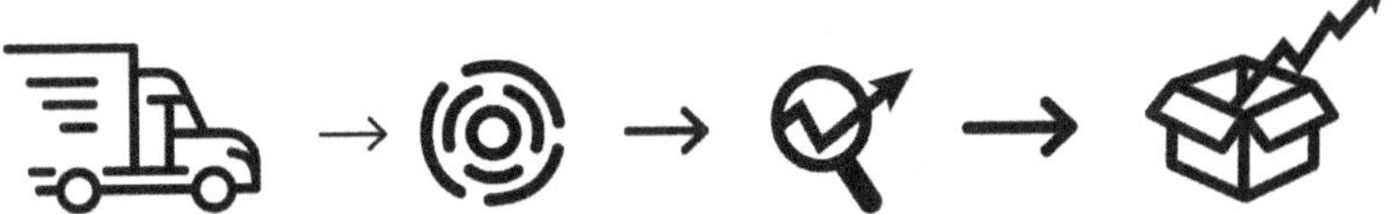

MOVERS MARKETING

A NO B.S. GUIDE FOR MOVING COMPANIES TO WIN ON GOOGLE & MAXIMIZE ROI

TRAVIS WEATHERS

FOUNDER AND CEO OF ROTATE DIGITAL

DEDICATION

Behind the work of this book and the 10 years of experience is this amazing woman, my wife Meg. I first dedicate this book to you.

Second, to the Rotate Digital team, you are absolute ninjas and the best of the best.

GET IN TOUCH

🌐 www.rotatedigital.com

✉️ team@rotatedigital.com

📷 Instagram: @travisweathers

TABLE OF CONTENTS

YOUR DIGITAL OIL FIELD AWAITS

Let me tell you about the biggest opportunity staring you in the face right now—one that most moving company owners are completely missing.

Every month, millions of people search Google for moving companies, typing in "money" keywords like "movers near me," "moving companies," and "long distance movers." They sit there in front of their computer or scrolling on their phone, with their credit cards ready and moving dates already picked. They need what you're selling, and they need it now.

> Here's the problem: Most of these searchers will never find you.

Instead, they're finding your competitors—the ones that have figured out how to show up at the top of Google Maps, whose websites actually sell instead of just existing, who've claimed prime digital real estate, all while you've been focused on everything else.

This is about taking over the market share in your city and leveraging tools and online strategies to ethically steal leads from your competitors and funnel them into your pipeline so they can turn into revenue. If you ignore this battle and succumb to ignorance and complacency, you'll set yourself up to fight an ongoing battle of always wondering where your next lead will come from. OR you'll watch your competition walk all over you, and enjoy the plundered revenue that could have been yours.

Why This Book Exists

I didn't write this book to turn you into an SEO expert or a marketing guru. Frankly, you don't have time for that, and it's not worth your effort anyway. You're running a moving company, not a digital agency.

I'm giving you a way forward that you haven't known about until today: **the owner's playbook for leveraging Google without losing your mind or your focus.** No B.S., only insightful tactical knowledge that you can leverage to win on Google and maximize your ROI.

You need to know what matters, what doesn't, how to get maximum results, and avoid complacent, mediocre marketing agencies.

Think of it this way: You don't need to become an oil engineer to strike oil. You just need to know where to drill, what tools to use, how to tell when to pivot to find a loaded reservoir, and how to tell when you've hit something big.

Google Is Your Oil Field

Google is the world's largest oil field. But instead of oil, it's filled with prospects ready to use your moving company.

Every search for a moving company is a potential gush of revenue. Every person typing "movers near me" is ready to spend $1,000, $3,000, $5,000, or more on your services.

> The oil is there. The demand is massive.
> The profit potential is unlimited.

Just like oil drilling, you need the right strategy, the right tools, and the right approach. You can't simply throw money at Google Ads and hope for the best. You can't build a website and pray people will find it. You can't ignore Google Maps and expect to outperform companies dominating it.

> You need to be strategic and drill in the right spots. And when you hit that digital oil well, your business will flood with leads and the revenue you've been dreaming of.

What You'll Learn (and what you won't)

This book will teach you:

- Which digital real estate spots on Google actually matter for moving companies.
- How to turn your website into a sales machine instead of a digital business card.

- The Google map domination strategy that could triple your visibility overnight.
- How to run profitable Google Ads without wasting your money on useless methods.
- Lead attribution systems that show you exactly where every dollar is working.
- How to prepare for the AI revolution that's already changing search results.

What this book won't do:

- Turn you into a technical expert.
- Waste your time on tactics that don't move the needle.
- Overwhelm you with theory that you can't use to take action.

The Stakes Are Higher Than You Think

The digital divide in the moving industry grows wider every day. You might think that generating leads is the only goal that matters. It's not. Just turn your attention from generating leads for a minute and think about what's really at stake: generational wealth. With the right tools to make it happen, you can concentrate on creating a business that works for you without burning your energy to survive—one that can benefit your family for multiple generations.

Take action on the knowledge I am laying down in this book, and you'll grow to revenue numbers you've never thought possible. Ignore the tactics I've provided, and you'll lose your market share to competitors, run a negative-profit company, and end up shutting your doors or selling for pennies on the dollar.

Start Now

Apply these marketing insights and this playbook for your benefit. Don't waste 10 years of your life trying to become your company's "marketing guru." Instead, become the CEO who uses these tactics to buy back your time and generate new leveraged revenue. I've written these industry-tested methods to cut straight to the point, so you can actually reach your marketing goals.

Moving companies that will win over the next decade won't be those with the biggest trucks or the lowest prices. They'll be the ones that claimed their digital oil fields, beat out their competitors, and learned how to extract maximum value from this book.

Your digital oil field is waiting. The question is: Are you going to claim it, or are you going to watch your competitors profit off the opportunity you ignored?

7

THE FOUNDATION

Chapter One

THE OPPORTUNITY

As owners, we may understand the value of real estate, especially those properties that generate a predictable monthly cash flow. We may invest in properties, equipment, and teams, expecting a return—and we should. But there are two assets most moving companies overlook, even though they can generate tens of thousands in booked revenue every month: **Your Google Business Profile and your website.** Optimizing these two assets is the difference between having a thriving business or fighting for leads for the rest of your business career.

What I am about to share with you is how to leverage Google's ecosystem to make more dollars and enlarge your digital footprint.

These two critical elements that can explode your business aren't meant to just be used by your marketing team; they're digital *properties* that can generate thousands and thousands of dollars—*ten, twenty, fifty thousand dollars a month* for you. In the online world, **Google is the ultimate digital real estate platform.** It pays to know all about it.

Whenever someone searches for a mover, Google determines which "properties" (Google Business Profile(s) [GBP] and website[s]) appear at the top of the page. Like physical real estate, the most visible and highest traffic locations are the most valuable.

Whether we're talking about nailing the top spot on Google Maps, securing the first result in organic listings, or grabbing the lead position in a Local Services Ad, think of each placement as a digital storefront. The more valuable your placement, the more customers you'll have wanting to engage with your services. Here's the lay of the land.

Google's ecosystem is made up of multiple real estate zones:

- **Local Services Ads (LSA)** – Pay-per-call listings show at the very top.
- **Google Ads (PPC)** – Paid search results that appear and rank just below LSA.
- **Map Pack Listings** – A Google Business Profile located inside Maps.
- **Organic Search Results** – Website listings appearing below the maps.
- **Footer Ads, Knowledge Panels, Snippets** – Additional visibility zones scattered throughout the first page.

Your mission is to dominate these zones and turn a profit. This book will help you do just that. Do you accept the challenge?

The Edge You've Needed

This book is your tactical playbook to unlock the full power of your online assets and dominate your market.

You'll learn how to:

- **Turn your Google Business Profile into a local lead machine.**

  Get found on the Map Pack, generate more 5-star reviews, turn visibility into booked moves, and "steal" more moves from your competitors.

- **Turn your website into a sales machine, and get ranked on Google.**

  From layout to calls-to-action to photos, you'll build a website that turns clicks into calls without overcomplicating the experience. You'll get the information that works for moving companies doing $40 million a year and bring it into *your* business. Can you imagine how that would move the needle?

- **Rank higher on Google without wasting money.**

  Master SEO strategies, including keyword mapping, content creation, and backlink building, designed specifically for movers.

- **Use PPC and Google Local Services Ads the smart way.**

  Know when to layer in paid traffic, how to bid profitably, avoid common money-wasting traps, and quantify your exact ROI. Spoiler alert: You are probably blowing your money on this, and you're not even aware of it.

- **Track your leads like a pro.**

  Connect marketing and sales data to see exactly what's working, kill what's not, and invest confidently.

- **Adapt to the AI-driven future of search.**

  Learn what's changing, how to future-proof your rankings, and how to show up more prominently on tools like ChatGPT and Perplexity.

> By the time you finish this book, you'll know how to stop guessing and start owning your market one high-converting keyword, location, and customer touchpoint at a time.

It's Time to Build a Legacy Company

Opportunities in the Google Land are endless and life-changing. I'm talking about tapping into generational wealth and a new lifestyle! If you're like me, no one handed you the keys to the kingdom. You're building your empire brick by brick. Google is your shot to build faster and turn your digital real estate into:

- Booked moves
- Bigger margins
- Long-term security
- And lower your CAC (customer acquisition cost).

Mastering Google is your opportunity to build your kingdom! All you have to do is accept the keys. I am giving them to you right now. So, reach out, and take them!

Fair Warning: What you don't claim, your competitor will. But lean in to this Google opportunity, and your fields will be plentiful for the harvest. Ignore it, and it *will* have a massive equal and opposite impact on your business, your life, and your family. We all have to keep up in this ever-evolving world. If we don't adapt, we get left behind.

That's why I wrote this book. I want you to beat your competition, grow your business, and transform your family legacy while creating generational wealth. I know the pain of starting a business and trying to keep it afloat.

> Wouldn't you love to sleep soundly again? Wouldn't you love to stop worrying about your business' longevity and where the next lead is coming from?

Turn the page, and let's get started learning how to take your business to where you've always dreamed it could be. I know it can be done. We've done it for hundreds of moving companies. Let's do it for yours.

Chapter Two

GOOGLE'S DIGITAL REAL ESTATE

In the moving industry, your online presence determines your lead flow and consistency, the kind of clients you serve, and how valuable your moving company is on the market if you decide to sell.

The right tactical marketing strategy can put your company at the top of the search results in the highest visible traffic placements. Failing to rank above your competitors in your market means that all leads, sales, and revenue will flow to them. And if you are a competitive SOB like me, then you will want to do anything in your power to stop that!

SEO is about more than rankings. It's about getting the right traffic and converting it into paying customers. Whether you're a local moving company, long-distance mover, or specialty moving service, your success depends on one factor: Being found by the right customers at the right time. That means you must do everything in your power to ensure you rank high on Google. No one will be able to find you if they don't know you exist.

That said, I would be doing you a disservice to only write about SEO without talking about the bigger picture. The more you maintain and optimize your location, the more right people you will attract. There are layers to this strategy that allow you to access the bigger marketing machine available to you. I will teach you everything I know about it to help you get the results you want.

> At Rotate Digital, we've helped hundreds of moving companies nationwide grow their revenue through proven SEO and PPC strategies designed exclusively for the moving industry. We don't believe in one-size-fits-all marketing. Every tactic we use is backed by data and customized to your unique business, market, and growth goals so you get results that will actually increase your bottom line.

Now, let's get down to business and learn about:

- The different real estate spots on Google.
- How to leverage these spots for your business.

Before we dive into the lay of the land and Google's coveted real estate spots, let me share with you an insight about Google SEO and marketing. SEO is not really about rankings. It's about showing Google that your company is more valuable than your competitors.

The good news is that you already run a great company that deserves attention. Your customers know this (that's why you get so many referrals). But the problem is … Google does not know this. Google is always questioning the value of your business. *Is this a valuable company, and should it be included in search results*? You have to show Google that you are here to stay and are worthy of having visibility on Google!

Think about Google's business model. Google's customers (aka, you and me: the googlers) are the focal point, and Google wants its customers (us) to have the best experience and results when we search for products or services we need. That keeps the Google gods happy. To give googlers the best experience when searching for a moving company, Google uses a complex, secretive, and unique vetting process to present on a silver platter the best and most relevant moving companies. Google wants to match people with the right companies to provide them with the optimal experience. Your one job is to get Google to value your company so much that it will elevate your rankings in search results.

You might be the best mover in your city with the best trucks, the best team, and the happiest customers. None of that matters if you can't communicate that value to Google through your website, your reviews, and your content. Failure to do this allows your competitors to enjoy the leads and sales that should be yours.

Warning: I could write an entire book on each of Google's sections, the process, how everything should be arranged, and all the boring details in between, but your job is not to be a marketing expert; your job is to leverage these real estate spots to your advantage.

These are the five real estate spots to leverage:

1. Google LSA
2. Google AI (Gemini)
3. Google PPC
4. Google Maps
5. Google SERBM

I'll explain on a high level what each of these is and then go deeper on the tactics to leverage them in a later chapter.

1. Google Local Services Ads (LSA) – The Verified Goldmine

Like "goldmine" implies, LSA equals prime real estate on Google. It ranks as the #1 spot because it shows up at the top of Google above traditional paid ads (PPC), the Map Pack, AI Overviews, and organic results. When someone searches for "movers near me" or "moving company," Google LSA shows up first. But you can't just pay for it and appear there. Google doesn't allow just anyone to access LSA.

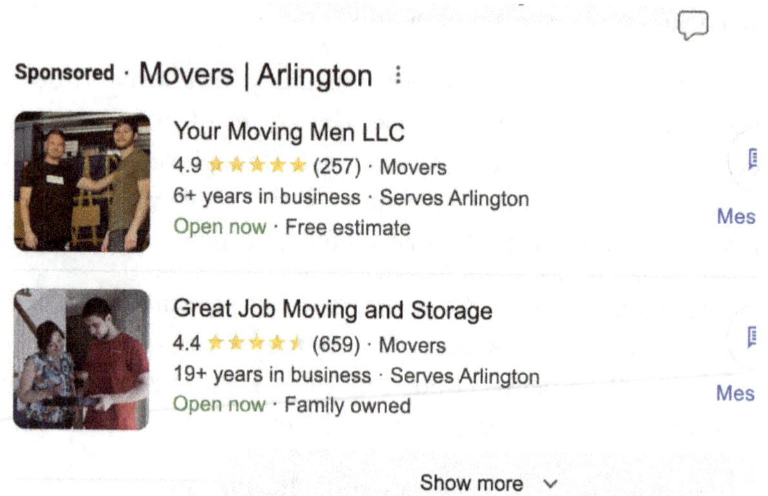

Here's an example of what an LSA looks like.

To advertise through this premium paid strategy, you must have a Google Business Profile (GBP) and apply to Google to use it. Your application process is a vetting process. Once you've applied, Google will conduct a background check on you, verify that you have state minimum insurance, and that you are licensed in your state and can legally operate your business. It's a bit of hoop-jumping, but it's a tough vetting process because rogue movers can't get access, giving *you a competitive advantage.*

You don't pay for clicks with LSA, unlike traditional PPC. You pay for calls. Real leads. People who are ready to move, not just tire-kickers clicking on ads. Every time a real lead calls you through this platform, you are charged a premium fee, but spending a bit more is worth it because you're reducing your spam. Simply take the call, do your sales magic, and book them! If any call is spam or doesn't fit the definition of a lead, e.g., someone looking for a job, you **do not** get charged.

For the lowdown on how to do this, check out Chapter 6 and the bonus strategy that VERY FEW companies are using. I'll explain how you can leverage it to your advantage, enabling higher closing rates and better ROI.

2. Google's AI Overview (Gemini) – The New Authority Builder

Google Gemini is Google's AI search results. When Gemini is triggered, it shows up below LSAs but above the Maps AND SEO search results. The Gemini results are considered prime real estate. Currently, it's dishing up a lot of content based on searches, like someone looking for "top rated moving companies in XYZ city" or "cost of living in XYZ city," etc.

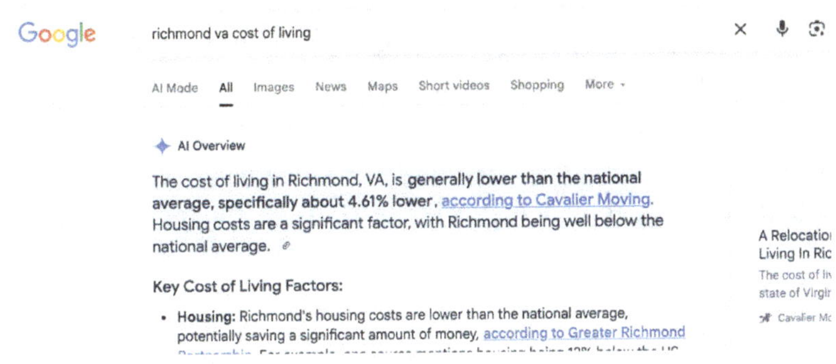

Here's an example of Google Gemini results.

When Gemini pulls data to answer a question, it chooses what it thinks is the most trustworthy. When someone types "how much does it cost to move a 3-bedroom home in Atlanta?" Google's AI Overview summarizes the best answers on the internet and provides the answer within seconds.

Very few websites get the honor of being used as a source for these answers. If your business is one of those, it gives your brand a huge value lift, helping your SEO rankings. Becoming a more valuable business to Google drastically helps your success in rankings.

3. Google Paid Ads (PPC) – "The Most Sophisticated Auction"

Welcome to the most sophisticated auction of your life.

With Google paid ads, you bid on keywords. Google assesses your value and brand, your website, your traffic, the time of day, location, a searcher's history, competitiveness, the number of bidders for the keywords, the top price companies are willing to pay, and the ad quality content to decide who gets placed in these spots.

Google uses sophisticated software and code in the bidding process to create an intricate auction between businesses. Often, if the criteria are similar, the winners awarded impressions and clicks are those willing to pay the most. Google PPC allows you a presence in cities where you might never have ranked. Remember, you are paying for clicks, not calls, although calls are the desired outcome from those clicks. Keep in mind that because you are paying for clicks, the risk of spending money on irrelevant traffic significantly increases.

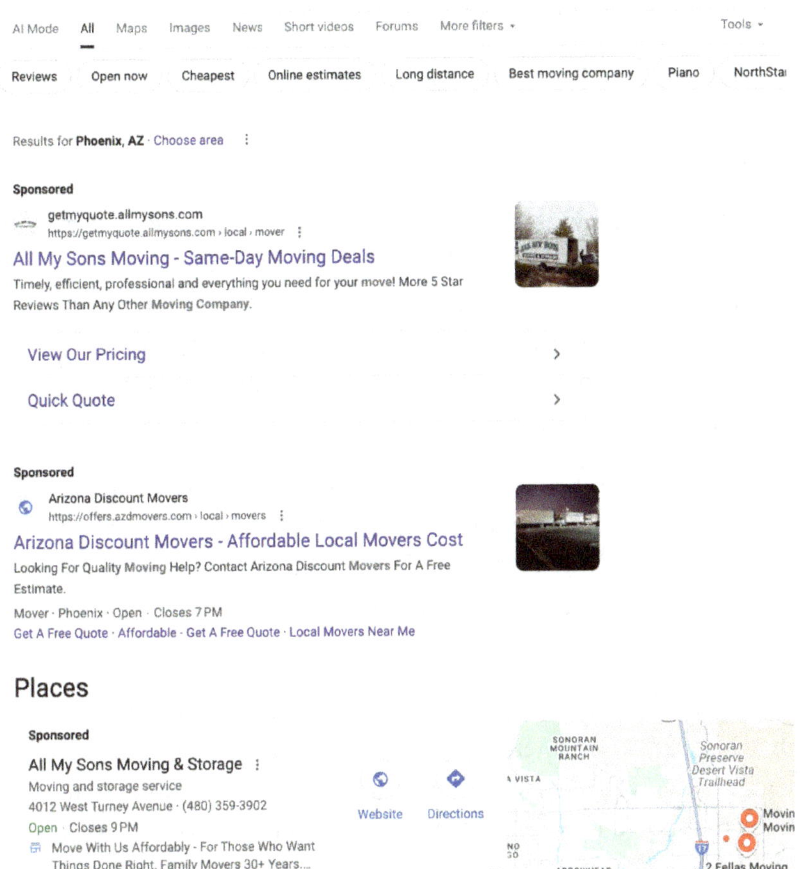

Here's a screenshot of Google PPC results on the first page of Google.

Most companies are wasting tens of thousands of dollars a month on this channel, hoping it will drive real revenue to their business. In reality, it's not doing anything for them. Sadly, PPC has become a cesspool of marketers scamming moving owners out of money and results. In Chapter 7, I'll share more on how the scams work and what you can do to avoid them.

4. Google Maps – The Local Trust Engine

Google Maps is the **most powerful** zone for moving companies, hands down. I have actually dedicated an entire chapter to it because there is so much value waiting for you as a business owner.

When you are visible in the top three spots on the Map Pack with competitive reviews, BOOM, you'll get an instant influx of leads! Because people trust the results in Maps with stellar reviews, they make a decision with a single glance. Google Maps is an owner's dream, offering you a huge opportunity to drive more leads and box out your competition.

I will teach you a specific strategy to dominate with higher leverage and a faster return on investment that I brought to the moving industry in 2021. We still use it at Rotate Digital today to drive higher results for our clients. You can read more about it in Chapter 5.

I'll conclude this section by sharing a motto for Google Maps that I hope you'll remember: "If you're not in the **top 3** of the Map Pack results, you're invisible to your prospect and thus revenue and leads that could be yours will go to your competitors until you show up."

5. The Google SERBM – Your Website's Battleground

The final real estate spot is what I call Google SERBM—a term I made up that stands for: **Search Engine Results Below the Maps**.

The more common title is "organic results." You'll also hear it referred to as SERP results (Search Engine Results Page).

In the search engine results below the map (SERBM), you'll only see results from your website pages. Unlike the Maps section, where your asset is your GBP, this section uses your website as the asset. It dissects your site, grabbing your homepage, location page, service pages, blogs, etc., and places them on the search results.

SERBM results vary daily, and although they will change depending on geographic location, these SERBM results have fewer proximity restrictions, which is your competitive advantage to leverage.

There's a major barrier to these results that is not often discussed with you when you're paying for SEO that you need to be aware of. I'll dive into how to win ranking battles that matter, avoid messing around with rankings that don't convert, and stop wasting money on this real estate section in Chapter 4.

The Opportunity

These five critical digital real estate spots on Google all have value, all serve a purpose, and can ALL be used to bring you more leads and a return on your investment.

But you can't do any of this without a website, so that's what we're talking about in the next chapter.

Chapter Three

YOUR WEBSITE IS A SALES MACHINE, NOT AN ONLINE BUSINESS CARD

Most moving companies treat their website like a digital business card. Static. Passive. Decorative. Boring, like a non-descript, budget-friendly hotel. Do you remember the last economic hotel you stayed in? Was it impressive? It probably just seemed like all the other hotels.

But what about that luxury hotel you treated yourself to that one time? It cultivated an experience. You paid a premium to stay there because of that.

Your site needs to care about your client's experience, like that luxury hotel experience. When you do this, you can drive up your prices, create more trust than your competitors, and book more moves. With a few adjustments, your website can become one of your most valuable digital assets and an extension of your sales team.

In case you think you need a site with all the bells and whistles, slow down. Your website can reflect your current business status without hindering you. If you are a startup with doors barely open, you don't need the "gold standard" website. Just get your business out there so it looks legit and allows you to focus on growing it. Once you get out of the beginner stage, you'll have more time and money to make your website a sales machine.

> In this chapter, I'm discussing the "gold standard" goal for your website, so you can identify when it's the right time to make the needed changes.

Everything I am sharing with you in this chapter is to help you bring in more money with your website. It starts with turning your website from an outdated business card to a fierce sales machine.

The Purpose of Your Website

Your website serves two purposes: First, it sells for you—it's an extension of your sales team. A properly positioned website effectively sells your brand, company, service, value, and trust to prospective customers. That's your primary goal. The second purpose is online visibility. It should rank for sales-relevant keywords and drive traffic and leads to your business.

I'm going to break down the **non-negotiables** to make your website a sales machine. In the next chapter, we'll talk about how to make your website rank better on Google.

Sales-Focused Website

Because the only thing worse than no traffic is traffic that doesn't convert, we need to create a sales-focused website.

I'm providing you with a list of what you need to do in order of priority. You can go right down the line and check off each item as you go. There are thousands of things you can do in marketing; the key is doing them in the right order and at the right time. If you have the money to do so, you may be able to accomplish *all* these to-dos; if not, you can still make a difference by prioritizing your actions and tackling the list from top to bottom.

1. Professional photography.

Have you seen these guys before?

My lord, I've seen them everywhere.

Here's another example of two moving dudes you've likely seen before. Stock photo garbage at its finest.

The problem is that stock photos like these are on 50% of moving company websites, and …

- These are not your movers or your uniforms.
- This is not your brand.
- Those aren't your trucks.
- Most importantly, it's not YOUR company, and consumers know that.

If they don't feel like this is a real company online, do you think it increases or reduces your prospect's trust in you?

Fake-n-bake photos tell your prospect: "We don't care enough to show you who we *really* are, *and* don't care enough to show you real photos." Guess what? Boring experiences and brands cause companies to lose a minimum of 10-20% of leads. And it's so preventable.

Let me hit you with something wild.

> According to research, websites with authentic, professional photos convert *45% better* than those using generic stock images.[1]

That's almost double the engagement you can have, just by swapping out those cheesy stock photos of grinning strangers for real, genuine photos of you and your team.

Putting legitimate photos of your real crew and trucks on your website forges an emotional connection with your visitors. When they feel like they know you better, they feel comfortable picking up the phone and calling you.

Fake photos throw up unnecessary objections and cause emotional disconnections with your prospects, causing you to lose out on leads and revenue.

---

1   Ackerson, Matt, and Name. "How Images Increase Conversion Rate [an Update]." Growbo, July 4, 2025. https://www.growbo.com/images-for-highest-conversion-rate/.

The photo below is on All My Sons' website and has been there for years:

Do you think that this half-a-billion-dollar moving company randomly selected this photo? Absolutely not. They strategically used a smiley little boy to create an emotional connection to the brand, knowing that this child's face on their site would make people feel good and trust them. But imagine if they used a stock photo like this instead:

You might be laughing at this, but most movers have photos like this on their websites!

Here's the solution: Skip the stock photos, and hire a photographer for half a day to capture your team in action. Show your work, your people, and your brand, and create a connection the instant someone lays eyes on your website. You'll immediately separate yourself from your competition, increase your prospect's trust, and most importantly, increase your lead flow without doing ANYTHING else but replacing stock photos with professional photography.

We've now done this process with hundreds of moving companies and have built a checklist to help you get the kind of high-ROI photos that pay for themselves 20X over.

Scan the QR code or visit the website and download Rotate Digital's photography checklist. You'll see every type of photo you need, how to find a photographer/videographer, and view sample photos on websites that have been done the right way. You can literally hand the checklist to your photographer, knowing you will get the results you want!

Grab it at www.rotatedigital.com/book-downloads

Or use this QR code:

Bonus, Ninja-Level Stuff

Your prospects are not the only ones noticing these stock photos. Remember when I shared that your goal is to make Google believe that you are as valuable a business online as you are offline? Well … Google has the ability to read the photos, and it knows that they are stock pictures.

When this happens, it brings your credibility down. Just like that, you've earned negative points with Google. Studies show that real photos with real emotions correlate with increasing traffic and impressions—crazy to think your actual photos help your SEO rankings, too.

To get to the absolute ninja level of this tactic, take some professional photos of your crew and trucks in front of well-known landmarks. Since Google reads and analyzes every photo and knows these landmarks, it creates a stronger correlation to your city and your company, giving you a better shot of making your moving company more relevant in your city in Google's eyes, aka you will increase your rankings.

If you're ready to take your photography to this level, by all means, do it! But if you're not, do what you can. The goal is genuine professional photography if you're ready for it. Don't let this ninja hack stop you from just executing and getting these photos for your website.

2. Leverage reviews on your website.

I know you've been told repeatedly, "Get reviews!" We all have. But most of us stop at that. Our goal is to leverage the reviews for maximum ROI. You can make them so prominent that they are always in front of your prospect, so they can't forget how awesome you are. Users have a short attention span; within seconds, they are building a case for or against calling you. That's why you want to keep your reviews in front of them.

Below is an example of what your website should look like, with reviews that are impossible to ignore.

You want your prospects to be sold on the experience, quality, and consistency of your excellent service *before* they reach out to you. Don't just use a separate "Testimonials" page. Sprinkle your reviews throughout your website. Every major page should have at least one glowing review. Especially your homepage.

Bonus: Have your developer or marketing agency install a scrolling review widget, showing your prospect your Google 5-star reviews *everywhere* they go on your website. We institute this strategy for a majority of our moving company clients because it's such a valuable trust-builder. Any applicable widget works, but these are the ones we've used and like:

- Rich Plugins: www.richplugins.com/business-reviews-bundle-wordpress-plugin
- EmbedSocial: www.embedsocial.com/google-reviews-widget/wordpress/
- Review Slider: https://wpreviewslider.com/

3. Calls to Action (CTA).

A well-done and engaging website without strong calls to action is like a Ferrari with a governor on the engine. It looks fast and powerful, and people like to stare at its bombshell beauty, but under the hood, something is strangling its full potential.

That's what happens when your website lacks clear, well-placed CTAs. You've invested in a digital asset that could go 200 mph (or 321 kilometers for you metric system people), but it's stuck doing 60 mph in the slow lane because your customers don't know where to click or how to call and move forward; this is killing your conversions. Luckily, there's an easy fix for this problem.

When a prospect lands on your homepage, ready to take action, the next step needs to be unbelievably clear. If not, they'll move on, you'll lose the lead, and *you won't even know it happened.*

Data proves that our top-performing websites have, on average, five CTAs on every main page. These CTA buttons could read "Call Now" or "Get a Quote." Here are some examples.

As a bonus, use buttons that follow a user as they scroll on their phone. So, when a customer decides to act, there's no friction. They just click and take action.

You may be suffering from this "governor" on your website if:

- Your quote form or CTA is only located at the bottom of the homepage.
- You don't have a quote form or button to obtain a quote on the homepage.
- Your call-to-action is not immediately evident—users must scroll to find it.
- CTAs are buried in paragraphs of text.

Here's an example of the real impact of making your CTAs more evident and clearer: After optimizing CTAs on a client's website, they gained 24 more quote form submissions than usual. Of those, 70% were qualified, and 40% booked, equating to six new jobs and $7,200 in additional revenue. If those results hold steady over 12 months, that's over $86,000 that never would have hit their wallet.

That is the power of placement and meeting the customer where they are.

Pull out your phone or laptop, and check your homepage. Can you see a quote form or a "Call Now" button without scrolling? If not, that's your first fix. Next, scroll through the page. Are there multiple calls to action? If not, your customers aren't seeing them, and that's costing you jobs.

> You don't need to spend more money on ads or traffic. You don't need more SEO. You just need to give your users a better experience.

Most marketing firms don't focus on this recommendation. They push owners to chase more traffic, and they ignore the traffic that's already there.

Traffic doesn't build revenue. Conversion does. Every visitor who bounces because they couldn't find your quote form is a missed opportunity. You're paying for traffic—and sending it to a leaky bucket.

Bonus Action: Tell People You Can Text

Wherever your number is displayed, let prospects know they can text you, or put that information on the button itself. Make it clear that your company is available for text conversations. People are talking on the phone less and prioritizing texting over calling.

When I moved early in 2025, I called and texted seven different moving companies. Only one prioritized texting with me. Guess which one I built up the most relational equity with? Yep, the one that texted me back. Texting gives you another opportunity to win over customers and boosts the number of people willing to chat with you.

4. Clarify your message.

In his book, *Building a StoryBrand*, Donald Miller shares that one of the seven critical aspects of clarifying your message is making the process crystal clear to your customer or prospect.

You know the moving process like clockwork, but your prospect does not. If you skip explaining what they can expect, you put up unnecessary barriers between them and their decision to hire you.

Customers and prospects want to know what will happen when they move with you. This graphic does a great job of walking them through what they can expect from a moving company.

Moving companies usually have a pretty simple process. Present it well, and it will create confidence in the prospect to work with you.

Written out, your process may look like this:

1. "**Talk to Our Team:** Get a personalized quote that fits your move and your timeline."

2. "**Lock in Your Moving Date:** We handle the moving details, so you can focus on preparing for your next chapter."

3. "**Enjoy a Smooth Moving Day:** Our team shows up on time, clean and ready to safely move you into your new home."

This process is clear, short, simple, and focuses on the user's experience, not your internal company's workflow. It's about what *they* will get, what *they* will feel, and what *they* will accomplish.

Take 10 minutes today to think through your process from your customer's perspective. If you need to, adapt the one I've shared to your brand, and get it on your website today!

5. "Why Choose Us?" section.

If you've implemented everything you've read so far, you're already rising above your competitors. But if you are like me (a bit obsessive, lol), you want to make it even clearer to the user that <u>you are the best</u>. It's time to implement a "Why Choose Us?" section like the one displayed on the opposite page.

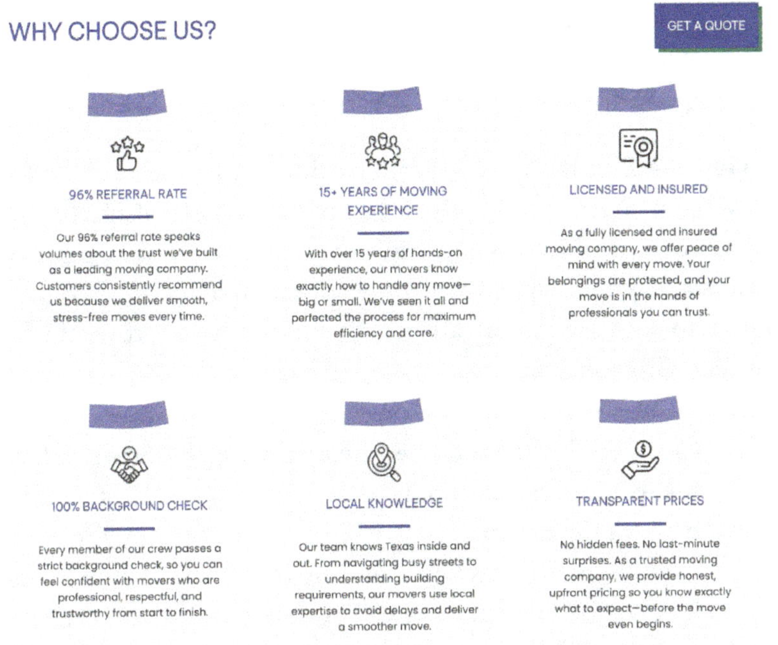

This section will uniquely separate you from your competitors and give prospects the confidence they need to choose you. In order to have the best "Why Choose Us?" section, you need to focus on two aspects: It needs to be real to your business, and share the benefits/outcomes with the prospect. It's about what they're going to experience when working with you.

Here's an example:

"We Conduct a 100% Background Check: "Every member of our crew passes a strict background check, so from the start, you can feel confident with professional, respectful, and trustworthy movers."

Not only is this real because you actually do background checks on your movers, but you've shown the prospect the benefit to them: They will have trustworthy movers in their house and won't be scared of people stealing.

Owner's Tip: If you are struggling through this section, here's a tip: What is routine for your business might be new, insightful, and helpful to your prospects and customers. Emphasize your signature services and values. Here are a couple of examples of what could be routine to your service and are great benefits to your prospect when working with you:

1. **Can pets be around the house during the move?** Maybe this is a normal occurrence for your team, and other companies might offer this service, too. But they might not be talking about it. When you beat them to the punch, your user might think no one else is doing it—by the sheer fact that you're highlighting this service. If it's important to your prospect, they will feel more excited toward your company, even though other companies also offer this service.

2. **What about sweeping up quickly after the move?** This is a great benefit to add to your "Why Choose Us?" list. Most customers loathe trying to find the extra energy at the end of a move to clean up. Knowing you've got them is needed reassurance.

As a gift, use www.rotatedigital.com/book-downloads or this QR code to download the 10 best "Why Choose Us?" points on your website.

6. Connecting to Your CRM.

The final critical piece to make your website a sales machine is to connect your quote form to your CRM. Streamline it so that your sales team can call any lead and speak to them confidently within five minutes of the prospect's information coming to you. If your leads are just going to your email, it will take longer for you or your sales team to reply, and by that time, you might miss the opportunity altogether.

Resist having a long quote form. No prospect has time to fill out how many couches and boxes they have. It's your team's job to find that out through the sales process. Capture the minimum viable information you need so your prospect doesn't leave your website because you are requiring them to do too much.

Below is a list of the minimum viable information that you need to capture from your prospect on your website.

Minimum Viable Information:

1. Moving From
2. Moving To
3. Move Date
4. Move Size (use house size or square footage, not truck size)
5. Name
6. Email
7. Phone number

I would be VERY hesitant to add any more items to this list because the more you include, the more barriers to entry you create for the prospect.

I've deliberately not included the marketing and UTM information (it's okay if you don't know what this is yet) because we are diving deeper into this in Chapter 8 on lead attribution.

Bottom Line

Above all, your website must be a sales machine. Notice how in this chapter, I didn't talk about SEO, URL structure, or SEO items for your website. That's because too often, owners get caught up in SEO talk before they've even explored how their website can sell. It's essential to implement SEO in your website, but it's secondary to creating a website that is a sales machine. Your website is not an online business card. It should be **your hardest-working sales rep**, selling, converting, and collecting data that helps you grow 24/7, that never sleeps or asks for a raise.

Most movers leave tens of thousands of dollars on the table because their site is bland and not unique to them. You now have the blueprint of core items to transform your website into a sales machine.

In the next chapter, you'll learn how to leverage your new sales-focused website to achieve killer SEO results. Let's get into it now.

GOOGLE ORGANIC

Chapter Four

SERBM RESULTS
(SEARCH ENGINE RESULTS BELOW THE MAPS)

You've learned about the importance of a sales-focused website, how to achieve solid social proof, branding, photos, and all that jazz. Now, we're going to address *how to get on Google using your website and how to rank for keywords that MATTER.*

Like all good solutions, there are steps to the process and traps marketing companies can get stuck in (and drag you into) that you need to be aware of. This chapter discusses how to leverage your website for maximum visibility on search results below the map.

You need to know:

- What are the search results below the map, and how can you leverage them?
- What are the keywords you want to rank for?
- How to structure your website to get maximum visibility.
- How to avoid the merry-go-round of wasting money on search results that don't matter.

The aim of everything we are talking about in these few pages speaks to one purpose: *Pushing Google to value your business, know who you are, what you do, who you serve, and where you are doing it.*

To get there, you must leverage your website in these three ways:

- Create the necessary and critical core pages for your website.
- Use URL page structuring on your website.
- Apply a blog strategy that puts your website in the top results of sales-relevant keywords.

What Are Search Engine Results Below the Maps?

Easily stated, unlike PPC or LSA, SERBM are organic results that you cannot pay to appear on.

Google results occurring below the Maps section occupy over 50% of Google real estate; your placement gives you the opportunity to dominate top spots and drive tons of relevant prospects to your website.

Results below Maps are pulled from specific pages on your website and act as a lever to push you to appear in Google. The key to your success is appearing on Google for sales-relevant and commercial-intent keywords. This is why you need to care about the content and structure you are putting out there on your website.

Sales-Relevant Keywords

The most effective way to drive the results you want is to enable your pages to rank high on the search results for sales-relevant keywords.

These are keywords your prospects are using to search for a mover when they're ready to buy. It's easy to rank for keywords, but the game you're playing is to rank for these most valuable keywords that will drive the most revenue to your business. Here's the list of the core keywords you want to focus your SEO efforts on:

- Movers
- Moving company
- Movers near me
- Moving company (your city)
- Movers (your city)
- Movers (your state)
- Moving companies near me
- Long distance movers
- Commercial movers
- Best moving companies
- Moving company near me
- Moving services
- Local movers
- Moving help
- Local movers near me
- Movers and packers

Notice that these are all commercial- and sales-intent keywords, comprising the exact phrases people choose when searching for a moving company. You might notice that we're not getting into keywords like "top cities to live in (city, state)," for example. Why? Because *they are not your target keywords* ... BUT they have their place and purpose. I'll share more on that in the blogging section of this book.

There are two important spots on your organic search results: Your Gemini search results and your results below the Maps.

Google Gemini Results

Google Gemini results have an amazing benefit for you.

1. Gemini results pop up in the top part of Google results, aka in the prime real estate area.
2. If you appear in this section, you'll have more visibility, driving greater awareness of your brand.
3. Most importantly, when Gemini picks you, it means that Google values your brand.

The most important benefit of Gemini plucking your information to blast out to users is that it means Google values and trusts your business so much that it is pulling from your content to populate its results. A Gemini result equals a boost in SEO rankings because Google sees merit in your business and wants everyone to know the content you put out. This is a leading indicator of SEO results.

> You can use any kind of SEO ranking platform to check how you are performing on Gemini. My company, Rotate Digital, uses Ahrefs to view clients' Gemini terms ranking. We'll dive into AI results and how to get more of them in Chapter 9.

Core Critical Pages for Your Website

If you want to rank on the search results below the Maps, keep in mind that everything will be pulled from the pages and content on your website. To be successful, you must have core pages and structures.

Since we have built over 300 moving company websites, garnering top Google rankings in almost every major metropolitan area, you can trust that this list of pages will help you achieve the ranking outcome you are looking for.

Homepage

Your homepage is critical for the Google algorithm. It is the page that shows up when someone visits your company's domain, such as:

www.yourmovingcompanyurl.com

In short: You must have a homepage focused on your brand and company.

Service Pages

Another critical *group* of pages is your service pages. Each service you provide, or at least your main services, should have its own dedicated page that describes the service and its benefits through both content and pictures. Your service pages are an asset for Google to understand what you offer.

Of course, people will find your service pages on Google. I am not denying that. But from a holistic point of view, service pages are mainly used for getting Google to understand what type of company you are, what you offer, and what value you bring to the table. Google then filters your search results to determine if your company will show up.

For example, if you specialize in piano moves, build out a service page around that, so when somebody searches for piano movers, Google sees that your website is relevant to that search term. When all the outcomes and pieces come together, you'll be promoted to the search engine top spots for piano movers—all because you constructed a beneficial and individual service page around piano moving.

One of our clients was a partner with Steinway & Sons, a store selling pianos. You better believe we leveraged that client's partnership to the fullest, including applying Steinway's logo and backlinking to their website, as well as using content and photos to create the piano-moving service page. *This one page earned them the #1 ranking spot* for "piano movers" (for Charlotte, North Carolina), in both search and on Maps' results. Here's the best part: Because of this ranking, this company increased its piano moves by over 400% that year.

Service Area Pages

Service area pages are another required critical batch of core pages that have the same purpose as service pages and make Google aware of your services and specifically where you operate.

Focus on your core locations. If you are a smaller moving company, build two to seven core service area pages first. Just as you did with service pages, construct these pages with content, photos, and city information. Including this content will rank you relevantly higher in your city when someone is searching for a moving company in that area.

We coach our clients to be careful and strategic about the number of pages they create on their website. Google will penalize you if you have service pages with zero traffic. Many owners think they need to create a service area page for every single city they can think of. It's a clever idea in theory, but the danger is, if you create all these service pages and don't have a strong enough brand to produce traffic for every page, you will get dinged! Pages with no traffic diminish your brand value to Google, causing potential ranking positions to dip.

If you are a larger brand, you have the freedom to create a lot more pages at once and not risk a dip in rankings.

> **Bonus Tip:** Take professional pictures specifically for each city page and display them on your service area pages to gain extra relevancy in Google's eyes.

About Us Page

An About Us page contains content about the company, the owner, the purpose, any charity or cause the company supports, and anything else a prospect needs to know that sets the brand apart. Google uses this page to understand the personification of your brand—so make sure you focus on your brand's uniqueness.

Contact Us Page

You want to show Google (and your clients and prospects) a specific way for people to contact you. Keep this page simple. A contact page removes barriers for your prospects and shows Google you are open for business.

FAQ's: Frequently Asked Questions Page

The FAQ page is one of the most omitted pages on a moving company's website, but it's really important to Google and you! Number one, it helps your sales process. It provides a way for your prospects to find out answers to the common questions they have when looking to book with your company.

The other undeniable reason why we force all our clients to have a frequently asked questions page is that Google uses this page to assess the quality of your business. Google Gemini commonly pulls from this page, and any large, well-ranking moving company has an FAQs page. Follow their lead.

Bonus Owner's Leverage: One of the smartest ways to leverage your FAQ page is to publish the most frequently asked questions prospects ask on sales calls or those you get during the moving process.

For example, do you move propane tanks? You and I both know you can't, but your customer doesn't. Give them the answer on your FAQs page and link back to the DOT rules that you are legally bound to uphold. This kills two birds with one stone: You've answered the prospect's question, and you've demonstrated to Google that you are familiar with the rules and laws moving companies must follow. When Google knows this, it increases your brand's value.

Here's a visual of what I mean:

AI Overview

No, moving companies generally will not move propane tanks. Propane tanks are considered a hazardous material due to their flammable nature and are on the list of items movers typically refuse to transport. This is due to safety concerns and potential liability issues for the moving company.

Reasons for not moving propane tanks:

Flammability:
Propane is a flammable gas, and moving it in a moving truck poses a significant fire hazard.

DOT Regulations:
The Department of Transportation (DOT) regulates the transportation of propane cylinders, and moving companies may not have the proper licensing or equipment to transport them legally.

Things Your Mo
Lambert Movin
Jan 10, 2025 — Th
professional mov

Lambert Moving

Will Movers Mo
moveBuddha
Some movers will
precious items un

moveBuddha

VIDEO: Movers
Here's Why.

Some sample FAQ questions and topics you can answer and address on your page:

FAQ Topics:

1. Moving insurance.
2. Items you cannot move in the process.
3. Your company's overall moving process.
4. How you charge for moves.
5. Should you tip movers?
6. Do you take TVs off the wall?
7. Do you assemble or disassemble beds?
8. Do you work with Sleep Number beds?
9. Do you have to remove items from dressers?

Standalone Reviews Page

The standalone reviews page contains company reviews aggregated in one spot for Google to eat up! You'll include your Google reviews, but you'll also post your Facebook, Thumbtack, Angie's List, and BBB reviews, and any video testimonials you want. When you create this reviews page, Google crawlers independently assess your company's value with real people, making Google want to rank you higher.

Owner's Bonus: By including a direct link to your Google reviews, you establish another connection between your website and your Google Business Profile, helping your Maps' rankings.

Sitemap Page

Design a sitemap page for your website and link it specifically to the footer (bottom of your website). A sitemap is a treasure map for Google bots, giving them directions where to go and telling them what to look at when navigating and digesting your website. Having a properly built and submitted sitemap ensures Google can navigate your site without missing important pages. Your marketing person or agency should know how to execute this; if not, just Google "sitemap generator" and use one of the top results to create this page.

> **Disclaimer**
> For the accessibility page, privacy policy page, and terms and conditions page, please don't take what I am about to tell you as legal advice. The focus is on leveraging these pages to rank on Google.

Accessibility Page

The accessibility page shares your website's proactive commitment to making content usable for all visitors, including those with disabilities. It typically includes your accessibility policy or any guidelines you follow, i.e., Web Content Accessibility Guidelines. Include contact information for users to report barriers or request assistance. When Google sees your compliance, it adds more clout to your brand and builds your credibility.

Terms and Conditions and Privacy Policy

The Terms and Conditions (T&C) page is your website's house rules and liability shield. It covers how you operate and use data, allows you to set mandates, maintains your legal obligations, and may even make legal action a shorter and cheaper process. We advise our clients to work with their lawyer to create appropriate legal content for their T&C page.

While T&C is for house rules, the privacy policy page is both your data transparency page and compliance stance. These are mandatory pages to include for your best shot at ranking high on Google and to CYA (if you know what I mean).

Owner's Tip: If you don't want to pay a lawyer, there are many standard plug-n-play templates available. As your business grows, your liability will grow. Keep that in mind when making legal decisions.

I'm only bringing up these pages because they matter to Google and are key pieces that the Google algorithm inspects to determine how legit of a company you are.

If you have any more questions about the legality of what should be included in these pages, please don't email me. Talk to your lawyer!

Your Website's Footer Section

Many moving companies use their website footers as junk drawers of information, but your footer should not be an afterthought. It should be designed to flow with your brand. Google's crawlers view your footer as a reliable signal pointing to your most important pages, allowing a better understanding of your site's structure and authority. Below is a list of key items to include in your footer.

Name, Address, Phone Number

Include each location and its address and phone number in your footer. Make sure this information matches all your contact information outside of your site, since Google also takes uniformity into account. If your website does not list this essential data, it's harder for Google to understand who you are, where you serve, and what assets are yours.

Remember, if you have more than one Google Business Profile (which our best-performing clients do), you need to have a dedicated service area page for each location.

Social Media Icons and Community Badges

Finally, in the footer, provide all your most important icons, including your primary social media accounts. The top three icons in the moving biz are Instagram, Facebook, and YouTube. If you have more accounts, you can add those, but start with those three.

If you don't have any accounts on these platforms, then this is a perfect action item for you to go create one and link it to your website.

Share community badges and awards in your footer, but also put them on your homepage or About Us page. Posting your badges and awards gives you social proof, resulting in more Google relevancy points and consumer trust.

Blogs Section

You may not have blogs on your site just yet—especially if you are a startup—but ultimately, you will want to have a blog page and structure built into your website.

There is one great reason you'll want to build a blog section on your website:

> *It earns Google's trust when you create valuable content. And the place you build this valuable content is in your blogs.*

There are two ways to write blogs. The first way is by yourself or with your team. The second way is through your SEO agency. I'll share with you the tricks to writing valuable blogs on your own to build value for your company.

To write blogs with value, you must sit in the shoes of the reader. How can you provide the most value to them? The best way to do this is to write blogs based on the content of questions that come to your sales or customer service teams. There are two key benefits of doing this:

First, instead of answering questions on the phone or email, you send people blog links to read. This standardizes your team's response, creates faster efficiency, and provides a better customer experience. For example, someone may ask: "What happens if you break my stuff in a move?" You have the ability to send them a well-written answer via a blog, letting them know about your company's process and the legal requirements of 60 cents per pound replacement, while also sharing with them the risk and rewards of purchasing moving insurance, or excuse me, "valuation."

Second benefit: By writing this blog post and going live, you've officially created valuable content! Guess what? You've taken a great step to show Google that you provide value for its users, and your company is the real deal. You've also laid down the first stone to create more chances for all your other brand pages to increase their rankings. This is the crux of why most SEO agencies have some type of blogging or content strategy in their services. I'll jump into this more later on.

Owner's Ninja Hack: By writing this blog, you've saved your team time and created standardization in your company. Even better, your customer will click the link and spend a great deal of time reading it (because they want the content and answers), thus Google sees both the traffic and the extended time visitors are spending on your site, which signals that you have valuable content—potentially boosting your rankings.

> Here is the bottom line about having a blog on your website: Google wants to provide valuable answers to searchers. To earn coveted Google spots, create relevant, meaningful content for your prospects. You get double the value from one action with an optimized blog.

Pulling This All Together with the Right URL Structure

You now have the master checklist to create the best website for your company, prospects, customers, and Google. But that doesn't mean you can just randomly throw up these pages on your website like New Jersey did with its highway system. You need the right organization and URL structure to support what you're doing. Thankfully, you don't have to know any tech beyond what is required to install this structure. And you can literally hand this checklist over to whoever is at the helm of your website. It's that easy!

I'll use "yourmovingcompany.com" as the domain to keep it simple as we talk about the URL structure. Again, don't worry too much about understanding this, as it's a blueprint for whoever will do this for you. If you don't trust them to do it, call us.

- Homepage (yourmovingcompany.com)
- About Us (/about-us)
  - yourmovingcompany.com/about-us
- Reviews (/reviews)
  - yourmovingcompany.com/reviews

- Contact Us (/contact)
  - yourmovingcompany.com/contact
- FAQ (/faq)
  - yourmovingcompany.com/faq
- Service Area (/[your state]) (I'll use Texas as the example):
  - Top-level service area page
    - yourmovingcompany.com/tx
  - Service area 1: (/tx/dallas)
    - yourmovingcompany.com/tx/dallas
  - Service area 2: (/tx/plano)
    - yourmovingcompany.com/tx/plano
  - Etc.
- Services (/services):
  - yourmovingcompany.com/services
  - Service page 1: (/services/local-moving)
    - yourmovingcompany.com/services/local-moving
  - Service page 2: (/services/piano-moving)
    - yourmovingcompany.com/services/piano-moving
  - Etc.
- Blog (/blog):
  - yourmovingcompany.com/blog
  - Blog 1:
    - (/blog/top-5-citites-to-move-in-dallas)
  - Blog 2:
    - (/blog/deducting-moving-expenses)
  - Etc.
- Terms and conditions (/terms-and-conditions)
- Privacy Policy (/privacy-policy)
  - yourmovingcompany.com/privacy-policy
- Accessibility Page (/accessibility)
- Sitemap (/sitemap)

This is your foundational URL structure. You will potentially build out more pages and structure in the future, but if you've just launched your business, this list gives you the best odds to win the Google rankings and search results racket.

Stacking the Odds in Your Favor

Implement what you've learned, and Google will love your brand and value your company. You'll see it in the relevant search results it serves up to the thousands of people hiring movers every day.

Some of our clients have spent years doing SEO work with minimal or mediocre results. The moment we strategically build their website, following the exact protocol I detailed here, their results skyrocket through the roof—all because we've made it easy for Google's crawlers to index your website, understand who you serve, what you serve, why you serve, and where you serve.

When the right results hit and you strike oil, you'll fly up the search rankings and see a flow of leads coming to your business. Then your amazing team will lock your prospect into an estimate, and you guys can give them the move they deserve!

The top nationwide moving companies have been blown away by their soaring results, thanks to our proven structure and page list that Google currently can't get enough of. Now, it's yours to use as a strategic starting point.

If you're concerned, confused, or want to learn about more opportunities, feel free to reach out to me or anyone at Rotate Digital. We'll share with you what you've done well and the opportunities awaiting you if you decide to work with us.

Now that we've locked and loaded this profitable game plan that you're hopefully excited about, it's on to the next chapter.

Chapter Five

GOOGLE MAPS STRATEGY FOR MOVING COMPANIES

As a moving company business owner, Google Maps is one of your most powerful tools and assets. It can be a literal vehicle to generational wealth for your family and future generations.

Year over year, using the strategy I am about to teach you in this chapter, we have seen our clients double, triple, and quadruple their sales and transform their businesses. I can't stress enough the importance of learning how to accurately use Google Maps rankings with your Google Business Profile.

Rotate Digital was ahead of the game because we looked at this asset (GBP) differently than its standard "digital marketing" use. We turned over all the possibilities of how an owner could leverage its power and opportunity.

Let's start with some basics.

What Is a Google Business Profile (GBP) and Map Ranking?

Google Maps is another powerful real estate spot where you want your business to show up. It appears below LSA and PPC, but it gives you the ability to capture leads in the Map Pack rankings.

You can rank on Google Maps if you have a Google Business Profile. For the sake of keeping this holistic, I'm gearing the content in this chapter toward a moving business owner who already has a GBP. If you don't have a Google Business Profile, set that up now. There are plenty of YouTube videos that can show you how.

Although you will show up on Google Maps, located on maps. google.com, our focus for this book and as an owner is to show up on the Map Pack rankings that appear on the Google search results. See below for an example that shows up on page 1 of search results.

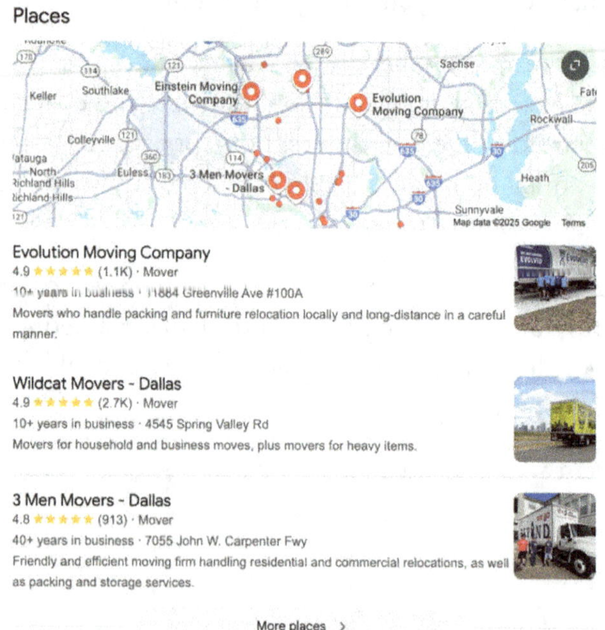

When someone googles a keyword such as "moving company," "movers near me," "long distance movers," "commercial movers," etc., a map based on the geographic location of the searcher will populate with Google's top choices.

> Google Maps throws up predominantly geographic, search-based results, and this is your strategic advantage.

There is one downside. You cannot rank in front of people if your Google Business Profile is not geographically close to them. But this is also your competitive advantage because you don't have to fight against major competitors like Yelp, Thumbtack, or Angi's list because they don't have physical locations in your area.

There are also numerous benefits. One is the ability to box out your entire competition based on your GBP being geographically closer to the searcher. This is great because if you have a major competitor, you can still beat them by proximity.

The second major benefit of the Map Pack ranking is that it offers review-based results, like you see for Amazon products. When you visit Amazon and type in a product you want, your results will give you the best sellers and products with the most reviews. Google Maps results heavily consider the reviews you have when deciding who will see you. This is fantastic if you have stellar reviews because a user wants validation for their decision on what moving company to use. And if you have great reviews, you validate and earn trust from the prospect before they even click or call you.

> Remember: Trust is the currency of the internet that you must leverage for your company.

How Owners Can Leverage Google Maps

Because Google Maps is a proximity plus reviews-focused asset, one of the most powerful ways you can leverage it is to get a ton of reviews. If you're wondering how many reviews are enough, here's a hint. When you're sitting in your office (or close to it), search some of these sales-relevant keywords: "movers," "movers near me," "moving companies," "commercial movers," and so on. You should show up on Google Maps' results in the first three spots because you're literally in your office or nearby (proximity). Your job is to be one of the top two reviewed businesses on those results. If you are not one of the top two best or most reviewed, there is a good chance you will be losing out on leads that decide to call your competitors. Your action then is to get more reviews. Strive to be one of the top two businesses reviewed in your area. That's the gold standard.

Diminishing Leverage on GBP Reviews: You should know there is a diminishing return on reviews. Let's say you're one of the top movers in your city with 500+ reviews. That's great, but if you continue to build reviews for this profile, you will have a diminishing return because you are already outpacing all your competition. Those extra 50 or 100 reviews won't bump your rankings meaningfully. If you get reviews on your profile faster than your competitors, you can leverage this edge to get double or triple your lead flow by gathering these reviews on an additional location. I'll share more on this secondary location later in this chapter.

Owner's Warning: You may be tempted to buy reviews, and there are certainly places just waiting to sell you the dream that you can do this. Don't fall for it. There is a high chance that Google will catch this, and the risk far outweighs the reward. In one sad case, our client, with over 300 five-star reviews, went ahead and bought 30 reviews even though we told them not to do it. Over the course of six months, Google caught wind. Not only did they suspend the profile, but they removed this client's entire Google asset—all because they'd specifically bought reviews that Google could prove were fake. Imagine forever losing your GBP asset, generating you tens of thousands of dollars a month in sales, all because you tried to buy reviews. Don't do it.

Owner's Hack: Get Google reviews with photos. Photo reviews help with the buying and trust-building process and also let Google know who you are targeting and where you're located. When a review with a photo is uploaded, a geographic stamp—or metadata explaining where that photo was taken—is included. If you're trying to rank in Gilbert, Arizona, and your photo reviews include geographic stamps all around Gilbert or the East Valley area, you are signaling to Google that you are a real and relevant company in these areas and have the data to back it up. You'll have a great chance of moving up the rankings and beating out competitors who do not have these photo reviews in their profiles. Great photo reviews also push down bad reviews. Win-win!

Optimizing your Google Business Profile

Physical Address or Service Area

Your Google Business profile gives you two options to use when setting up your account: a service area option and a physical location option. A service area option allows you to tell Google that you have a predominant service area in cities around you, without permitting Google to share the exact location of your office.

The second and preferred option is that you can show a physical address on your GBP, so searchers can see precisely where you are located. In the majority of cases, a real location with a real address will beat out GBPs with service area locations. This gives you the best odds to rank for more keywords, which will drive more leads to your business.

Owner's Warning: Often, we find owners with locations in "warehouse districts." This makes sense as you may have a warehouse, but the downside is these locations are usually in areas without a high population of people, or these areas make up lower-income housing—people who can't afford to move. Beware of this. You may rank well on Google, but if your right audience is not around your GBP, then you won't see the revenue you could potentially earn. Later in this chapter, I share a solution for you.

Your Business Name

The least risky way to name your Google Business Profile is to use the actual name of your business that matches as closely as possible to your LLC entity or DBA on file with the state. If you add the city to the backend of your business name (e.g., My Moving Company – Dallas), it *can* help you rank better, but you increase the risk that your profile will get suspended. Ironically, the only way to fix this (if this happens) is to go back and rename your business profile so that it matches your LLC or DBA option mentioned above.

Over the last five or so years, Google has worked exponentially hard on getting rid of fake profiles and locations. Google is getting increasingly strict about what it decides is a real location. It is doing this by getting granular with your naming profile details and making sure they are the same as the LLC or DBA on file with your state. They only want to show their customers (us "googlers") real businesses with real locations run by real people.

The Rest of the Details

You want your entire Google Business Profile to be fully visible, with all sections filled out with relevant information to the best of your ability. Key items to fill out include:

1. The description of your business (don't keyword stuff!)
2. The category
3. Services you offer
4. Physical address
5. Phone number
6. Hours of operation (the hours you will answer a phone call)
7. Areas served
8. FAQs

For more details on Google's Guidelines regarding representing your business on a GBP, check out this link to read more: www.rotatedigital.com/guidelines.

Your Google Business Profile is an incredibly powerful asset. Once the foundation of your profile is completed (competitive review rating, competitive number of reviews, optimized profile, and physical address), then you can create new "sales" locations to expand your visibility. I call this Google Monopoly!

When you have multiple locations, Google's algorithm takes this as a sign that the brand is valuable.

Google Monopoly

Your goal as a business owner is to dominate your major city, but since there is a geographic proximity restriction to your GBP, you must get outside the box.

If you only have one business location, you will have a hard time dominating large metropolitan areas. In fact, it's impossible to do that with one GBP. Just look at Two Men and a Truck in any major metropolitan city. What do you notice? They have multiple locations all across the area. Phoenix has six locations. DFW (Dallas-Fort Worth) has nine. Although Two Men and a Truck may operate out of each of these locations, you do not have to do this; you can mimic this domination with real "sales" locations.

To Google, one of the definitions of strong brands is having multiple locations. Once you have a solid domination of your first GBP in your area, your leverage is to open your next "sales office." Before, your one location wouldn't show up in this area, but by taking this step, your business can appear in the new GBP location to a whole new population of prospects actively looking for moving companies. In Google's eyes, this new Google Business Profile is a real location with a real office and a real space to work out of, but you don't need to dispatch out of there. This is your hack. Open another physical location (sales office—not some P.O. Box) and build reviews and authority for this GBP. By doing this, you double your visibility and become visible to a new population of searchers.

Here is an example below in Chicago:

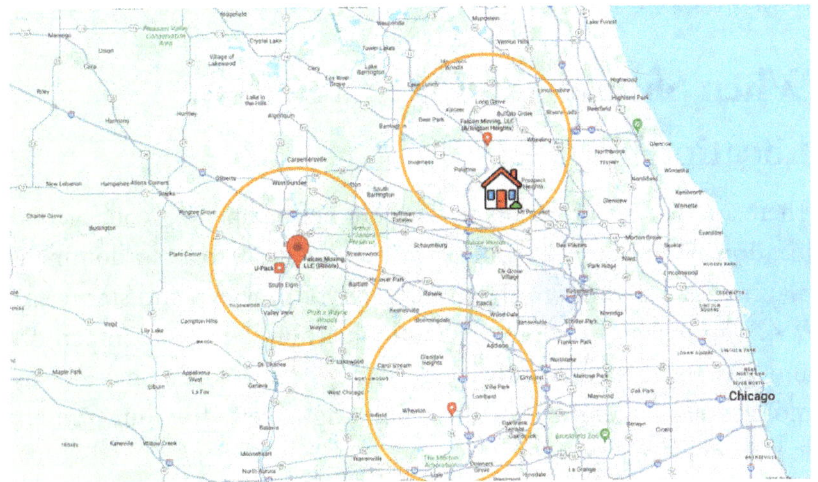

This owner started with one location in Elgin, Illinois, with an estimated five-mile visibility radius (shown by the circle). When someone in that circle types in any of the main keywords we discussed—like "movers" or "moving company"—this location appears in their search results. But if Grandma in Wheaton, Illinois, needs to move, she'll never see this moving company as an option because she's outside the visibility radius.

Strategically opening two additional locations—one in Wheaton, Illinois, and another near Prospect Heights in Northern Illinois— allows Grandma in Wheaton to see this Wheaton location and the reviews, call in, and book her move with this company! The same applies to a family googling "movers near me" while they sit in their home in Prospect Heights. You can see the immense value these additional locations bring!

The result? This company more than tripled the leads and sales coming to their business organically, all by playing the game of capturing real estate and visibility on the Maps Pack. This strategy helped them hit new revenue goals that would have been much harder to achieve with just one location.

When Should You Open a Second Location?

There are two major factors to consider before opening your second location. First, as I explained earlier, you need to be a dominant player when it comes to the number of your reviews and star rating (a 4.5 rating, for example). If you look around at your competitors and they have significantly better ratings than you or have vastly more reviews, then first focus on building reviews for your primary location before expanding.

Second, dominating Map Pack rankings for high-intent keywords in your primary location is non-negotiable. If you lack strong visibility on your first location, you won't see success with a second location. We want our clients to have 80% visibility for the majority of sales-relevant keywords, like: "movers," "moving company," "movers near me," and "local movers."

Visibility opportunity is unique to your city and competition—every area is different. To view where you currently stand, use the greatest tool out there, called Leadsnap.com, to see your market share visibility.

To have an expert do this for you, go to https://www.rotatedigital.com/visibility, and we will run the scans and share with you how well you rank for these keywords. You can also view my two-minute YouTube video explaining visibility with multiple locations. Check it out here: https://youtu.be/OUxerMeigPQ?si=uajiA-hR0O1BDw58

Choosing a Second Location

Identify a target city or neighborhood where you want to show up on Maps, then open a new office space or sales location there (again, as I explained earlier, it must be a real physical location you can prove to Google).

> We've found that Regus office spaces are great places to use for your next location because they usually give you everything needed to signal a real location in the eyes of Google—but at a fraction of the cost.

To determine a prime target location, one of the methods we like to use is the Costco strategy, which I learned from my friend Brian Yarham, a wonderful moving company owner.

Think about it.

Costco spends millions of dollars on research and development to figure out its ideal customer—a family in the middle to upper class that makes over $100,000 a year—and that's where they plant their Costco locations. If you follow that lead and establish new locations near Costco (or a similar-type company), you are literally piggybacking off their data, putting yourself right into neighborhoods full of your target customers.

> If you want more relevant data to help you choose a superior location, use a really cool platform called PolicyMap.com to access population data like annual household income, demographic breakdowns, and all the moving and housing information you could ever want.

If you want to learn more about the different types of addresses and locations you can choose for your next GBP, including the costs and risks involved, Rotate Digital has built a document that outlines your options and explains more. Download it here: https://www.rotatedigital.com/book-downloads or use the QR code.

GBP Map Pack Ranking Is Your Key to Fast Growth

If you take one fact away from this chapter, know this: Expanding your GBP visibility on Google search results (whether you have one or many locations) is the fastest way to get a return on your marketing investment. That's why the top moving companies all follow this process. Google Map Pack rankings with reviews build trust *fast*. People are moving their intimate, fragile belongings with you. They want to feel confident that your company has moved people successfully, and they rely heavily on the Map Pack results on a Google search to determine the moving company they will call.

It's not worth your time, money, and effort to spend thousands of dollars going after search results below the maps if you haven't first maxed out your visibility on your GBP locations. Don't ignore this asset and opportunity … Leverage it, and watch your leads flow in.

GOOGLE PAID ADS

Chapter Six

GOOGLE LSA

Welcome to pay to play, baby, where major private-equity-backed companies, companies with millions of dollars of marketing spend, go head-to-head with your moving company in a sophisticated, complex auction. It's a battle zone, and it's not built for you to win. It's built for Google to win—that's the game. You have to know how to play it in order to win and beat your competitors.

But how do you beat your competitors? How do you beat industry behemoths—and do it while not squandering your hard-earned money on Google? That's what I'm sharing with you:

1. How to spend money while tracking your ROI with 100% confidence.

2. How to get on the path you want. We hear owners say things like, "We tried Google Ads, and it didn't work," or "I don't know what leads or revenue is coming from Google Ads." If you're one of those owners, don't worry, this chapter (and a few others) will set you straight.

3. How to understand and uniquely leverage Google LSA and traditional Google PPC to spend confidently.

4. And the one huge benefit of Performance Max campaigns you can use to land on coveted Map Pack results.

I'll let you in on a few key points to be aware of, common misunderstandings when executing this marketing, where to focus your attention, how not to get scammed by agencies, and more. Let's jump into LSA.

LSA (Local Services Ads)

We'll resume our conversation around Google LSA by reminding you of what was shared in Chapter 2.

Google LSA:

→ Appears as the #1 spot above all other Google results—it's true prime real estate.
→ Requires Google approval through background checks, insurance verification, and licensing (your advantage).
→ Has a vetting process that keeps rogue movers out, giving you a competitive advantage.
→ Has you pay per qualified phone call, not per click.
→ Doesn't charge you for spam calls and non-leads (like job seekers).
→ Connects you with people ready to move, not just browsers.

Here is the deal. LSA is meant to be an exclusive marketing platform that you can use out of the box as an owner. It has call tracking, call recording, and a list of every lead that comes through this channel, all of which make it an easy experience for you to run on your own without a marketing person or agency.

On top of this, the Google approval process creates a built-in trust factor that consumers are drawn toward. It gives them the confidence that you are a better company to work with.

One downside to Google LSA is that you don't have the ability to customize your ad(s) or how you show up. It's all in Google's hands. Google determines the exact way it wants your business to show up, and when and how it does. This is the biggest limiting factor to Google LSA. Although this downside comes with the benefit of an easy user experience, it can be an issue for you if you want customization (you get that in traditional PPC, though).

The trick to your success comes down to tracking this channel's leads from the call through to your CRM—so that you can get an exact ROI from your ad spend. Any bad leads or spam leads can be disputed with Google to get your money back. This makes it a powerful platform for quick results.

Here's an example of what you must do to win with LSA. You will get the old lady calling, wanting to move her couch. You will get the calls about a 1-bedroom apartment move. And this will drive you up the wall and make you want to stop altogether, but remember, you will also get the family moving across the country, calling and asking you to move their house for a job relocation. You'll get the 5-bedroom luxury house move. You'll get the bigger moves you want, and you will find that, despite a few low-quality leads, your ROI overall is profitable.

Owner's Hack: The Google stamp of guarantee given when you gain approval from Google is a leverage point that you can use in your sales process and on your website. VERY few companies are using this to their advantage. Imagine that there are two moving companies: you and someone else. You seem to offer the same quality to the prospect, the same amount of good reviews, and you're both priced similarly. Now imagine that you're leveraging the Google

Guarantee badge (soon to be renamed Google Verified badge), and on your sales call, you share with the prospect that you have gone through a strict vetting process by Google. You share that Google has investigated your business licensing and insurance and performed a background check. Google has put its "Google Guarantee" badge behind your company name. As soon as your prospect learns this, you build extreme trust in their eyes and give them more security in your service. You've just massively embedded trust and authority into your company, and you can use this on *every single call to your business,* even if it didn't come through Google LSA.

> Put this Google Guarantee stamp on your homepage, in high traffic areas on your website, and use it in your sales process, and you'll close more jobs than ever before!

When you combine Google LSA with traditional Google PPC and SEO, you get extra visibility on prime real estate spots. You are seen everywhere, your brand trust skyrockets, and your competitors' calls drop. If you implement all these tactics well, you could essentially have prime real estate spots in all three coveted areas: LSA at the top, Google PPC below that, and organic SEO. This means you could literally dominate every real estate spot on Google's first-page results, leaving the prospect no other choice but to call your company.

Chapter Seven

TRADITIONAL GOOGLE PPC

Google PPC, specifically Google Ads, is hands down one of the most misunderstood tools in the moving game. If you're a moving company owner, like the other owners out there, you might be lighting your hard-earned cash on fire. I'm talking tens of thousands a month down the drain because you either don't know what you're doing or some agency is scamming you blind. But every downside has a flip side: When done right, this channel can absolutely drive major revenue to your business.

Note to the Reader: This chapter is not about how to set up campaigns. That would be a book in itself. If you want to do it yourself, YouTube has many videos on this topic. Instead, I'm covering the most critical aspects and insights you need to win the game and not be screwed over by agencies.

In our industry, it is extremely tough to be profitable in Google paid ads, but it's possible! It requires exceptional setup and intimate management of campaigns, clarity of your COGS (cost of goods sold), and, super-importantly, an effective sales process. All these must be tuned just right if you want to turn a profit. The risk of not doing this is massive.

The sobering reality (don't let this discourage you!): Rotate Digital has found that 75% of the time, companies are wasting tens of thousands a month on this channel, hoping it is driving real revenue to their business. But in reality, it's not doing anything for them. Let me share with you a real-life story.

One moving client came to us, spending $40,000/mo on marketing, $32,000/mo in Google Ads, and $3,000/mo on the agency fee to manage that spend. They thought their Google Ads campaign was "working" because they had about $100,000 a month in sales from Google and wanted us to improve it. We jumped in and installed our lead attribution system and found that the reality was far from what they wanted. We accurately lined up the leads and sales in their CRM to the marketing campaigns, specifically separating out sales from Google organic and Google paid ads, and discovered that their $100,000 in sales from Google was actually comprised of $80,000 a month in organic Google sales; $20,000 in monthly sales came from paid ads.

Let's put this in perspective: $20,000 a month in sales with a hard cost (COGS) of each move of 40% meant that they were only getting back $12,000 in profitable sales from $35,000 in paid ads (spend + management fee). It was a total loss of the company's money, all because their previous marketing agency had set up a poor Google Ads campaign, wrongly focusing on a low cost per click instead of proper conversion tracking, ignoring proper lead attribution, missing out on leveraging their PMax campaigns, and not implementing OCT (offline conversion tracking)—information I am about to share with you in just a few pages.

Had they been aware of these problems earlier, they could have stopped spending money on paid ads and put $420,000 back on the company's bottom line for that year! On top of that, almost $100,000 was lost in hard costs on all these unprofitable moves. That's over half a million dollars of recaptured annual profit.

> Your takeaway? Doing Google Ads incorrectly can be the difference between companies scaling profitably and those operating with negative net cash flow.

Sadly, PPC has become a cesspool of marketers scamming moving owners out of money and results. We are going to change that today!

We will go through:

1. Overview of PPC.
2. Dangers of cost per click (CPC).
3. All about Google Ads conversions.
4. Critical metrics you need to track for PPC.
5. Your responsibility in sales execution.
6. The secret hack for PMax campaigns.
7. How agencies scam you (my favorite part).
8. Your checklist to reach the gold standard PPC execution.

Google PPC Overview

Google PPC is the ultimate pay-to-play system. It's a massive auction with hundreds of variables. Google looks at everything in this auction: your brand value, website quality, competition levels, time of day, cities you are bidding on, searcher history, bid price, landing page, and much more.

These variables give you more control over when and how you show up on Google—unlike Google LSA, where your hands are tied for 90% of the process.

A huge benefit, outside of some sweet Google real estate spots, is the ability to activate PPC, no matter if you are a startup company or a 10-year business veteran. You can spin up a campaign to gain visibility in spots all over your state and in specific cities, even if you don't have trucks or offices in that area. You don't need to be geographically close to the spots you are bidding on, either. You have complete control over how you show up, where you show up, what shows up, and what you are willing to pay to show up.

Dangers of CPC (cost per click)

Cost per click is a misleading KPI. Many people think cost per click is the most important metric in the Google PPC game. I see folks boasting on Facebook: "My PPC provider dropped my average cost per click from $25 to $5." They announce it without knowing anything else outside of that number. They're putting too much weight into it. CPC is simply a lead KPI measurement, meaning it's helpful to determine *if* your ads will be successful, but it's not *the* determining factor. Don't base your success on this number. It cannot be your most important number as an owner, despite the heavy focus many marketing agencies place on it. That's child's play.

Why Cost Per Click is Misleading

The cost per click number can be easily manipulated. Since it's able to be manipulated, scammy agencies take full advantage of this. For example, you could run a PPC campaign focusing on display network placements, but you would never really know the results because it's difficult to track garbage traffic, although it does drive down your "cost per click," making it look sexy and easy for your agency to celebrate with you on a monthly call.

The Real Danger of Low Cost Per Click

I know you will have this knee-jerk reaction to drive down cost per click, but tread carefully. Remember, keep your eye on the prize. The prize is quality lead conversions into your CRM. CPC is not the outcome you want to focus on. If you misplace your focus to solely drive a low cost per click, you may actually be boxing yourself out of valuable traffic and leads that could drive real revenue. Congrats to you if you got your cost per click down from $20 to $5, but at what cost? You may have lost valuable traffic and quality leads, and now, you are further from where you want to be.

> If you focus solely on a low cost per click, 95% of the time, only Google wins, taking your money and giving you back useless traffic.

So, if cost per click is misleading and not the number you should care about, what critical numbers do you need to know? Great question. These are the two critical numbers you need to know about: 1) cost per conversion, your Google PPC platform's most important number, and 2) return on ad spend (ROAS), your business' most critical number.

Cost Per Conversion: The Platform's Most Important Number

When talking to your marketing agency, put Google Ads cost per conversion on the agenda—this is Google's spit-out metric declaring how much you are spending to get to your desired Google conversion goal. Conversion is when a searcher goes from click to desired action. The key is to know where your conversions are happening.

Where Your Conversions Occur

You might be surprised to learn how easy it is for your agency to fabricate a Google Ads conversion. You NEED to ensure that your PPC provider, your Google Ads manager, knows the definition of conversions and can provide that list to you. Is it a phone call? A phone call click? A website chat started? A quote form submission? Does any phone call count as a conversion? You can see that a clear definition of conversions must be created and that both you and the marketing agency need to agree on it.

Don't forget: These conversions can be manipulated. Your agency could tell you that a conversion is a phone call, but without phone tracking and recording software, it may just be a phone call click. What do you consider a genuine sales opportunity for your business? Is it a 10-second phone call that times out? A 30-second call that never receives a return ring? Is it a one-minute hold, or someone calling and hanging up before somebody picks up? You might have your own definition, which is totally fine. **What's important is that you determine your definition of a conversion.**

Here is a list of core conversions we use for almost every client:

1. Phone calls lasting over 60 seconds.
2. Quote form submitted to the CRM.
3. Chat form started (if applicable).

> *Anything less than 60 seconds on a phone call is measured but not tracked for a conversion.

Use this as a foundational starting spot to ensure your marketing company is tracking proper conversions with Google PPC.

> **Insider Info:** At Rotate Digital, we track phone calls with substance, so we tell Google that phone calls over 60 seconds are a valuable conversion. Many agencies leave out this specification and just count any phone call—spam or fake. I'm sure you can see the problem with this.

Avoiding the Ambiguity Trap

Whatever you do, refuse to live in an ambiguous world of just blindly hearing about "conversions" without understanding what they mean. Your report needs to include: 1) exactly what is defined and tracked as a conversion, 2) how many conversions occurred, and 3) where the conversions occurred.

Over and over, we see owners saying, "Well, I have 125 conversions from Google Ads." Yet, when we dive in, there are only three leads in their CRM from Google Ads. Be intentional with your goals. Make it your responsibility to know what's going on with your numbers. Be informed. Tell your agency the conversions you would like to see. You might say, "I don't want to build my account on five-second phone calls or forms that weren't completed."

Know:

- Your campaign goals.
- How your goals are defined.
- What data you're feeding back to the Google algorithm.

> Google is all-knowing; it knows what people will buy, who will buy, and when they will buy, all before they know they will buy it.

The Game-Changer: Offline Conversion Tracking

Many marketing companies skip one particular tactic, called offline conversion tracking (OCT), causing a detrimental impact on your business. Without OCT, Google treats every form submission and phone call equally—whether it's a spam call or an $8,000 booked move.

With OCT, you feed back to Google only the conversions that actually turned into revenue, then Google's Smart Bidding AI software learns to find more valuable leads that you want for your business.

The difference is massive. Instead of optimizing for volume, Google optimizes for profit. Your lead quality skyrockets, cost-per-booked-job drops, and you stop wasting money on tire-kickers who were never going to hire you.

One of our clients didn't use OCT when they started with us. Once we implemented proper OCT, their invoiced return on ad spend (ROAS) hit 7x their spend. This means for the $6,000 they spent on Google, they returned $42,000 in booked moves from Google Ads! That's the power of teaching Google to be smart about your business, instead of allowing it to throw random leads at you.

Owner's Warning: Many agencies miss two critical steps when building a PPC campaign. First, they don't send conversion data back to Google, allowing it to go rogue and run up any type of conversion—good or bad—so their metrics never improve. Make sure your agency is uploading your conversion data back to Google.

Second, agencies upload **any and all** conversion data. This instructs Google: "Do more conversions" without telling it what conversions are the RIGHT ones. You can literally show Google your optimal conversions and the prospects you want to see interacting with your brand, so Google dials in better people to advertise to.

This subject goes deeper than you can believe. If you upload buyer conversions, Google may be able to take that data, check out the income level, the credit card purchase history, the avatar, etc., all details that will then drive more quality conversions.

Consequences of Poor Conversion Tracking

If your cost per conversion is executed poorly, you will spin your wheels and spend your cash for too long, an unfortunate result of the Google Ads algorithm gobbling up your crappy data.

An example of what happens when poor conversion tracking occurs can be seen with one of our clients we took on in early 2025. In the first quarter, they had spent $93,000—for that spend, their marketing agency was reporting 14,000 "conversions." Of course, when we dug into it, we found there were only 100 REAL LEADS in their CRM for the business to try and sell and close. That's abysmal. That's $930 per lead (not per booked move, just for a lead), all due to poor conversion tracking. The owner had to deal with the fact that they were wasting money on Google Ads and not turning a profit. We fixed it with proper conversion optimization.

What to Watch For

When you're looking at the Google Ads platform, pay attention to the cost per conversion. You should see the metric progressively drop after day one of implementation—an indication that the Google Ads process is going well. When cost per conversion is dropping, it means your cost per acquisition is improving, which increases your ROAS—your true north star metric.

Return on Ad Spend: Your True North Star Metric

As an owner, the most important number in your Google Ads performance is return on ad spend (ROAS). **You won't find this metric on Google Ads.** You need to create it yourself. It is your most important number because it allows you to track all your spend, conversions, and your true ROI. If you pull it all together, it tells a story of how your Google Ads investment is returning to you.

The concept around this number is simple. You need to know:

- How much money did you spend on Google?
- How many booked moves did you get?
- What was the total revenue from those booked moves?

The answer to these three questions allows you to calculate your ROAS. But if you haven't executed and fixed what I covered earlier, you cannot figure out this number.

Calculating Your ROAS

Here is the formula for ROAS:

$$\text{Total Invoiced } \textit{Revenue} \text{ from Google Ads} \div \text{Total Spend on Google PPC} = \text{ROAS}$$

An example:

- You spent $8,000 on Google Ads last month.
- You received 80 legit conversions (calls and forms) from Google PPC.

- Of those 80, you closed 20 of them.
- The total invoiced revenue of these 20 jobs was $32,000.
- Your Cost Per Acquisition (booked job) = $400.
- Your ROAS = $32,000 ÷ $8,000 = 4X ROAS.

This means that for every $1 you spent on Google Ads, your return on investment was $4 in revenue for your business. This is your north star metric.

Improving Your ROAS

What's your baseline ROAS today? If you don't know, get calculating. To get your final ROAS number, measure back to the exact conversion, tied directly to each lead in your CRM. You may do this on your own, your agency may do this for you, or you may have a VA handle this task. No matter what, it MUST be calculated, or you will keep gambling with Google Ads. Don't forget: Google will win if you gamble your money and skip tracking your data with a fine-tooth comb.

Using the example above, a 4X ROAS is good performance, but you can improve it! Now that you know the number, work with your Ads provider to bring it up. Instead of 4X ROAS, how can you get it to 8X or 10X? Focus on systematically increasing that return month over month.

Fun Fact: We perform this feat of full circle analysis for you, so you don't need to worry about it. We step into your CRM, and our team of analysts ties every lead, conversion, booked job, and revenue back to Google Ads. With this info, our clients know if their ROAS and ROI are winning or losing.

Setting Realistic Expectations and Timelines

After figuring out your conversion tracking and ROAS baseline, work with a marketing agency to do everything you can to bring your cost per acquisition down and your ROAS up every month. Don't expect to see movement in just two or three weeks. Give it time to move toward the result you want.

You will see fluctuations depending on the demand, the season, and how well your sales team is performing. Over a course of three months, you should see steady improvements.

Your Responsibility: A Winning Sales Team

Take a moment and try to be ready to hear some hard truths. Without a good sales team or a dialed-in sales process, you're essentially throwing money down the toilet. Your sales team can make or break your successful investment in Google Ads. Google Ads leads are expensive and highly competitive. Many prospects don't trust you (yet) and will call multiple other companies when looking to book a mover. This means that you're starting off the sales call in negative territory, not neutral. *You must earn their trust to win their business.*

The clients we see getting consistent, positive ROI to win with Google Ads all have one thing in common: Their sales team is absolutely DIALED in. *You* must own this. Not your marketing agency, not your operations manager. YOU. You must fight weekly to make your sales team incrementally better.

Just this last month, I met with a client running Google Ads with us. Their return on ad spend was 0.5X. Horrible. They were losing money hand over fist, but when we looked at the numbers, they were on par with all our other winning PPC clients. Cost per click was healthy, click-through rate was phenomenal, and the conversion rate was within metrics. The difference? We opened up their CRM to find their close ratio was 3X lower than our standard clients we see winning (around 35%). Their team was missing calls, and they weren't following up with leads. It was chaos. This owner investigated and owned his messy sales process, which he had ignored for the last six months (we've all been there). Immediately, we stopped running all ads to save him money until he could fix the sales process. If this sounds like you, let me show you the two critical items to transform your sales process.

Two Things That Make or Break Your ROAS

The critical pitfall that kills your ROAS is a slow, lazy, and chaotic sales process. The brutal reality is that these PPC leads are hot and ready to book quickly. When prospects click on your Google Ads, they will either submit a form or make a phone call right then and there. If you don't answer, they'll move on to the next two or three businesses because they need to get "moving tasks" off their list. That's real life. It's a game of war between you and your competitors with Google as the battleground.

> To improve your sales process for increased ROAS, first, ANSWER. THE. PHONE. You cannot miss any calls. Period.

I get that it's a challenge, but you need to resolve this. Even the best companies miss calls, but they miss significantly fewer calls, AND they call back quick and use text messaging in the follow-up process. Most moving companies miss the boat and never use text. Meanwhile, these hot leads are open to have text conversations throughout the day. You're not replacing phone calls; you are communicating using their preferred method.

Second, speed matters. When a PPC form lead enters your CRM, you need to be lightning quick. Get on top of it, and shoot for a 30-second response time. Max out at a 5-minute callback window. You need the team, the personnel, and the system in place so that when a new lead pings, somebody in the office jumps on it like their life depends on it … or at least their commission check. Speed makes or breaks this game, and most companies are way too slow.

If you nail these two sales aspects in your sales process and combine that with a good closing ratio, you will be ahead of most of your competition. You'll be able to close more leads and successfully use Google Ads to scale your moving business.

Owner's Bonus: Create a separate workflow for your Google Ads leads. The top-performing moving companies are doing this exact hack right now.

Set up a different phone number (we use Whatconverts.com) that routes PPC calls directly to your highest-performing sales members. This small investment is nothing compared to the conversions you are paying for that your mediocre sales members are losing.

Hijacking Map Rankings with Performance Max Campaigns

I had to include a specific section on Performance Max (PMax) because it harbors a secret gold mine that, as an owner, you must know about. Performance Max is Google's "set it and forget it" campaign that spreads your ads across its ecosystem. We're talking Search, Shopping, Display, YouTube, Gmail, and Discover—every single Google property where ads can show up. PMax is Google's machine learning beast that automatically decides where to place your ads based on what it thinks will get you the best results.

Here's the gangster move most moving companies don't realize: PMax is your golden ticket to hijacking those precious Map Pack rankings. While all those other placements—YouTube ads, display banners, and Gmail promotions—are pretty much trashy traffic, Google Maps ad placement traffic is premium. This is what a Map Pack's ad looks like:

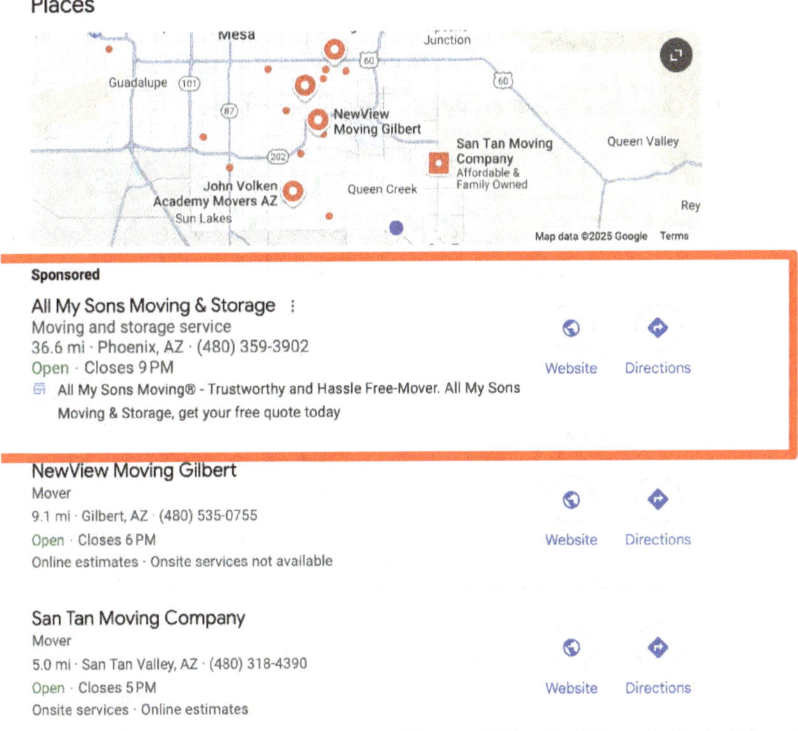

See that hijacking happening? PMax gives you access to this beautiful opportunity. These bad boys let you jump the line and place your moving company right at the top of the Map Pack, even if your organic ranking sucks. You're literally buying your way to the most valuable real estate on Google, where everyone's eyes go.

Here's the catch: Google won't let you cherry-pick and only bid on Map Pack placements. You've got to take the whole package, which means your budget will spread across all those other placements. We've run the numbers for our clients, and repeatedly, the results and conversions that come from this PMax bidding win every time. "Wasting" money on YouTube and display ads is still 100% worth it to gain access to those Map Pack ads—where you make the real money.

How You Get Screwed by Marketing Agencies

Secretive branded searches are the easiest way to bloat your Google Ads ROAS and screw you over. Branded searches are when your paid ad pops up on Google for *anyone* searching your brand name. Unfortunately, some marketing companies may try to secretly bid on your brand name, all to present you with the perception of better conversions and ROI.

We see this literally every month with our clients. People ask us to take over their Google Ads, and when we dive in, we find out they've got bloated data. Just this last month, a client's PPC account that we took over revealed that 75% of their conversions were coming from branded searches. We had to share the bad news that their "positive ROI" from Google Ads had been filled with conversions of secretive, branded keyword placements. The client had no idea this was happening! What they didn't know was literally killing their ROI.

Lazy and scammy agencies do this to show more conversions and better ROI. It makes you feel better about spending $10,000-plus a month on ads when the reality is that $8,000 of that spend went to spam and low-quality traffic, while $2,000 was spent on branded search terms that drove all the conversions (which you can argue would materialize as a conversion anyway).

When Should You Bid on Your Own Brand Name?

We find two good reasons to spend Google Ads money on your brand name:

1. You are competitive and want to take up all the prime real estate spots on Google.

2. You are combating competitors that are bidding on your brand name. Yes, this is allowed; it's a savage move, and it can be risky. But nonetheless, it can be done. And if you bid on your own brand name, since you own the brand, you will get a higher ad placement than any other company bidding on it.

Whether you spend money on your brand name or not, you need to be intentional with a purpose.

Here are some insights to protect yourself from scammy agencies:

1. Ask: "Are you bidding on my brand name for conversions?"

2. Let them know if you want to invest in branded keywords when someone searches for your brand name or if you want to stay away from it.

3. If you do bid on your brand name, make sure you have a separate and clear budget for how much you want to spend on it.

4. Ensure there is a clear separation of conversions from your brand-name leads versus "cold traffic" leads (people searching for moving services, not your company directly). This creates clarity in your ROAS, especially for the non-branded campaigns that need to succeed.

5. Hold your agency's feet to the fire. People are like electricity and follow the path of least resistance. Agencies are not immune to this. Set the (realistic) outcome you want and create distinction within your campaigns to be confident in your ROAS.

No matter what, be intentional—have a reason for whatever choice you make.

Wrapping It All Up

Google Ads is a BEAST, a "sophisticated auction going head-to-head with million-dollar companies and industry giants" kind of beast. And you can absolutely win this game if you play it smart.

> Of the three unique ways to get your ads in front of people, Google LSA (that pay-per-call system), traditional PPC, and Performance Max campaigns, each one has its place.

In this chapter, we dove deep into the numbers that actually matter: CPC, CPA, and ROI. But remember that final number you're tracking—ROAS—that is your true north star.

We also called out how agencies try to screw you over by bidding on your own brand name and padding their conversion numbers. Don't let them get away with it!

The Real Opportunity Here

I get all fired up about this section because I know what a difference it can make in your business, since most moving companies are operating their Google Ads completely wrong. They're wasting tens of thousands of dollars every month on garbage leads because they don't understand the game. But you? You now know exactly what to look for and how to win.

When you get these components right—proper tracking, a dialed-in sales process, and smart campaign management—Google Ads becomes a money-printing machine. You can dominate your current market more than ever before or even markets where you've never had trucks. You can outrank companies that have been around for decades. You can hijack prime real estate on Google with a click of a button, helping you scale faster than you ever thought possible.

The moving industry is ripe for disruption, and Google Ads is your weapon. Most of your competitors are still figuring out if they should even use Google PPC, let alone run sophisticated ad campaigns with proper attribution and sales processes.

Don't be one of the companies that "tried Google Ads and it didn't work." Be the company that figured it out, dominated their market, and left everyone else wondering how the hell that happened.

If you're already working with an agency, take this chapter and go to them. Ask the hard questions. Demand the tracking we talked about. Push for proper conversion definitions and separate reporting for branded versus new customer leads. If they can give you these things and show you real ROI? Great, you're in good hands.

But if they can't answer these questions or they get defensive? Then start thinking about what's next. Whether that's working with us at Rotate Digital, another agency, or building what you need in-house, execute these tactics to get the outcome you want.

The opportunity is massive. The tools are there. The only question is: Are you going to act or keep watching your competitors eat your lunch and steal your leads?

I'll leave you with this checklist to help you have a successful Google PPC experience. Use it. Share it with your marketing team or agency and check back often. Now, let's move on to setting up proper lead attribution.

Gold Standard PPC Checklist

Dial in Your Tracking with Your Team:

- Demand proper lead attribution from day one.
- Make sure every Google lead is tracked all the way to revenue in your CRM.
- Calculate your true ROAS and CPA, not just the platform metrics.

Fix Your Sales Process:

- Set up systems to answer calls within seconds.
- Respond to form leads within 30 seconds.
- Leverage texting to leads and prospects.
- Create special workflows and bonuses for Google Ads leads.

Use Performance Max:

- Be a savage and hijack the Map Pack rankings.
- Accept that some of your budget will go to other placements; it's worth it for Map Pack access.

Hold Your Agency Accountable:

- Ask if they're bidding on your brand name (if applicable).
- Demand clear conversion definitions (5-second phone calls do not count as leads).
- Separate branded versus new customer conversions in your reporting.
- Make sure that whoever is the liaison to the Google gods feeds good conversion data back to Google.

LEAD ATTRIBUTION AND THE AI WAVE

LEAD ATTRIBUTION: STOP WASTING YOUR MARKETING DOLLARS

In our modern age, you cannot run Google Ads or any marketing spend profitably without proper lead attribution. Ignoring lead attribution will be the fastest way to burn your cash and get nothing for it. Tommy Mello, CEO of A1 Garage Doors, a multi-hundred-million-dollar company, said, "Lead Attribution is my favorite word when it comes to marketing." He cares about this, and I care about this, so should you.

Lead attribution is a big phrase but a simple concept:

> Lead attribution is the process of identifying and assigning credit to the marketing channels that contribute to generating a lead or sale

You cannot afford to experiment with "conversions" without having insight into exactly what each conversion looks like—especially down to each lead in your CRM. If you want to win this game as an owner, you have to spend money (the easy part) AND track exact ROI to spend more or cut ineffective spending (the harder part).

Whether you use our system, your agency's system, or something else, you need to know exactly what leads are coming from what marketing channels.

Why Lead Attribution Matters

Your business is way too important to throw any money away. Period. Most clients come to us spending anywhere from $5,000-$30,000-plus a month on paid ads and SEO in the hopes they will get a return. Sadly, it never happens.

Remember that story in the previous chapter about the company that wasted over half a million dollars a year on poor PPC management? Well, that could have been avoided with proper lead attribution.

At Rotate Digital, we built out a complex process with AI technology so our clients can get all the lead attribution they need and know the exact ROI of their spend. This helps them make better business decisions and effectively get a return on their cash. If you want access to the tool and system we use, get more info at www.rotatedigital.com/book-downloads or access the QR code.

Is Confident Attribution Possible?

It doesn't matter what you have been told. The answer is YES, it is possible to have confident attribution. Not many companies have cracked this code because it takes time, effort, technology, and raw manpower to calculate, but we care so much about our client results and accurate data for ROI calculations that we built a system to make this a reality.

Bottom Line: Before you spend a single dollar on SEO and/or PPC, get your lead attribution system locked down. Know exactly what each campaign is bringing you; if not, you're just gambling with your marketing budget. Now let's dive in.

Lead Attribution Is Your Key to Profitability

If you do not get lead attribution correct in your business, you will always struggle to scale profitably. The keyword is "profitably." You may not always struggle to scale, but you will struggle to scale with money left in your pocket.

When you solve your lead attribution puzzle, you can scale quicker, maximize profits, and hold your marketing agency or person accountable. You have the ability to spend more money on marketing, complemented by data.

I'll show you what you need to know, how to get there, and how to scale profitably to keep more money. We'll move you away from the assumption model and into a presumptive model, based on data and probability.

The Three Fatal Mistakes in Lead Attribution

Before we tackle how to handle your lead attribution the right way, let me explain three mistakes most business owners are making.

Mistake #1: Bulk Calculations

Many owners use bulk calculations. They simply take the total marketing spend across all Google channels and divide it by the total revenue of all Google channels to get one lump ROI. They combine: Google PPC revenue with Google LSA revenue, with Google organic revenue equaling one "Google" referral source.

The problem is, when you rely on bulk calculations, you keep both underperforming and successful, performing channels in the dark. You have no idea what's working and what is not. Again, remember the story about the company that wasted over half a million dollars on PPC—all caused by bulk attribution.

Mistake #2: Leaving Out Key Data

The second mistake in lead attribution is leaving out key data. There are two key data points you want to include in attribution: 1) marketing UTM data, and 2) sales call data. If you are relying blindly on one or the other without marrying both together, you will fail to clarify what drove the lead to your business. This missing data can lead to faulty ROI calculations.

Mistake #3: Using Your Gut Feeling

If you rely on emotional gut feelings to drive your decision-making without using marketing and sales data, you'll fly blind with your business. And as a pilot and business owner, both are bad things to do.

The Solution: Three-Steps for Marketing Clarity

There are three pillars to installing *the* foundational lead attribution system:

1. You must integrate UTMs into your marketing channels.

2. You must capture your lead decoration, so it flows into your CRM.

3. You must combine phone data and marketing data to create an accurate report and build the "what's working" story.

Pillar #1: Integrate UTM Data Into Your System

You must integrate UTMs into your marketing channels. To do this, you'll leverage something called a UTM. I'm not going too deeply into the inner workings of UTMs because you can click the QR code below or access the link www.rotatedigital.com/utm and download an entire detailed blog explaining what they are and how they work.

UTM stands for Urchin Tracking Module—if you forget what it stands for, that's fine. I always do because what is important is how to use it. UTMs are parameters added to URLs so that you can decorate your website traffic from its last touch source. You will use a few main categories: Source, Medium, and Campaign.

Where Can You Use UTM Data?

You can use UTM parameters anywhere you have a link to your website. Some examples: Your GBP, a QR code, your postcard mailers, Google Ads campaign, a Facebook post, and many more places. See below for an example of how this looks on your GBP.

Without UTM tracking: If somebody finds and clicks "Visit Website" on your GBP, they will land on your normal domain URL: www.yourmovingcompany.com and fill out a quote form. Without implementing UTMs, your CRM would show absolutely **no** data about where that lead and revenue came from.

With UTM tracking: You can modify your GBP website link to include UTM data; see the UTM parameter (in bold) added below:

www.yourmovingcompany.com/**?utm_source=google&utm_medium=organic&utm_campaign=PhoenixGBP**

Now, when someone clicks from your GBP, they'll land on your domain page, with the UTM parameter attached. They will fill out the same quote form, *but now your CRM will include your marketing data*:

- Source: Google (they came from Google).
- Medium: Organic (this was organic, not PPC).
- Campaign: E.g., Phoenix GBP (the GBP they clicked).

The Result: Now you can attribute this lead and revenue directly to your organic Google SEO efforts. Instead of wondering where this lead originated from, you have the data to say your Google GBP generated a $4,000 move. This gives you a clear ROI on your local SEO efforts.

If you're not already doing this, your first action step is to install this UTM parameter to your GBP website link. Again, to get more clarity on this step, use the QR code or visit: https://www.rotatedigital.com/utm.

Pillar #2: Capture UTM Data Into Your CRM

With UTM data installed, you can now capture your newly decorated data and move it into your CRM. Lead by lead, you will know exactly where that person came from, if it was organically from Google, or paid from LSA or PPC, or another source—like a QR code on a truck, a postcard, etc.

Setting up this integration is an advanced step, so work with your CRM company and marketing agency to capture UTM data from the website, which will show up in your CRM. If this can't be done with your CRM, then be warned, it will be a nightmare for you to gain clarity. Currently, the Smart Moving and Supermove CRMs capture UTM data well, but many other industry-leading CRMs are quickly adding this feature for you (yay!). But even if your CRM cannot do this right, ***there is always a solution.***

Below is an example of a simple email to send to your marketing agency so that they can install this for you.

Email Template

> Hi <Name>,
>
> 1. Can my CRM automatically capture and store UTM parameters from my website? If not, what tools or integrations can help me track UTM data from my leads?
> 2. If yes, can you please make this happen for my website, so I can push UTM data to my CRM?
>
> Thanks!
>
> <Your Name>

This is your Trojan horse email because if your marketing agency responds that they do not know how to integrate UTM data with your CRM, or if they say it can't be done, it's a major red flag. If they say, "There's no good solution," then again, red flag.

There *is* a solution. It can be as simple as sending leads to both your CRM and a Google Spreadsheet with UTM data. If your agency doesn't have confidence in any aspect of this integration, I'd advise you to find a company *cough* Rotate Digital *cough* that can do this for you.

You need an agency with this technical know-how, and if this simple task is hard, then what else in their marketing efforts are they falling short on?

This is your second action step to ensure that your CRM is capturing UTM data on all form submissions.

Bringing It Together

Let's say someone searched "movers" on Google and found your GBP on the Map Pack results, then clicked on it to go to your website.

1. Prospect searches on Google for "movers."
2. They click your Google Business Profile link.
3. Because you've installed UTM data, they land on your page with decorated data.
4. Then they submit a quote.
5. The quote form populates your CRM, *now* with decorated marketing data.
6. The lead becomes a booked move for $2,500.
7. You can now attribute that $2,500 sale to organic Google SEO efforts (marketing spend), giving you ROI clarity.

Owner's Hack: I've shared all about capturing UTM lead data on form submissions, but what if these leads come to your website decorated with UTM data only to pick up the phone and call you? Out of the box, you'll only have marketing data on a form submission, but you'll completely miss *phone call* marketing data. Your solution is to install a phone tracking software on your website, giving you the ability to capture that UTM decoration from phone calls. We use WhatConverts.com, but you can use CallRail or any other call tracking company.

Pillar #3: Marriage of Marketing & Sales Data

To get the most accuracy on your lead attribution, you must create and see the story of each lead. You could look at marketing data alone, but you may be led in the wrong direction on attribution. Likewise, if you just trust your sales team and what they put into the CRM from phone calls, you'll miss out on the true accuracy of attribution. The best combination is to marry your marketing data with your sales call data. I'll share with you how you can get your sales call data, then I'll move into three different scenarios of how to analyze the data and attribute the lead to the appropriate marketing channel.

Collecting Sales Call Data

Since I've already walked you through decorating your leads with marketing data using UTMs, now it's time to decorate your leads with sales call data. Your goal is to capture what the prospect actually says about how they found you—what drove them to your business today.

Most moving companies gather this information by requiring their sales team to ask in the sales call, "How did you hear about us?" One solution is to use what your sales team puts in the CRM. However, you are relying blindly on the fact that your team is asking the question "How did you hear about us?" and that they entered what they found out into the CRM correctly. It's a method, but it's not a reliable method.

A better solution is to use a call recording software, either a native recording option with your phone provider, or use a call tracking number like WhatConverts.com; then you can have the calls recorded. Once they are recorded, you'll need to sift through the information.

You could have your sales manager listen to every single call or hire a VA to do the same thing. Either way, labor is going to be an uphill battle and costly. Instead, use AI for your solution.

You'll want to use a software called marketingclarity.com, which listens to the phone call and analyzes all this information. Using this AI solution allows you to assess sales call data and avoid spending thousands of dollars a month on humans to do this task. Instead, it gets done instantly when the call is finalized. The AI software can analyze the call to find out how the person found you, combine it with the marketing data, and collect information so you can make sure that all your sales reps are asking the question: "How did you hear about us?" It can also grade your sales calls and help you identify gaps and needs in your process.

> Now that you have marketing data and sales data,
> you can move on to using it to decide the "final attribution"
> for each lead.

Example 1: When Phone Call Data Trumps UTM Data

A user can visit your website via your Google Business Profile and submit a quote form directly to your CRM. That marketing data decoration will show the lead coming from organic SEO results through your GBP.

But what if, on a phone call, you learned that the prospect's friend, Mary Jane, had referred the lead? This would mean that this lead is ultimately generated due to the referral, not organic SEO, despite the marketing data showing otherwise. Your final referral source would be called a **referral**. You can only see this insight when you marry the marketing data and sales call data together to tell a story.

Example 2: When Both Data Points Align

Now imagine that a lead with marketing data is submitted to your CRM. The marketing data says that it's from Google PPC, and the call data noted that the lead mentioned they "found you online." With this information, you can confidently note that this lead is coming from Google PPC and that it represents a direct return on investment for Google paid ads.

Example 3: Your Data Can Be a Warning

Here's a **yellow-flag-raising situation** that indicates you should investigate further: Imagine a lead submitted from a PPC campaign (marketing data proves this), but on the call, they said, "Mary Jo referred me to your business." This is another example of a "referral" attribution. But marketing data shows that they found you via a Google ad. So, what does this mean?

It means that in the process of searching for your company, they clicked on one of your branded ads. Remember in the previous chapter when we talked about branded keyword bids? This example is solid evidence that you are spending money on your own brand name. If this is what you want, great! But if you do not want to spend money bidding on your brand name, you can explore your options.

When sales and marketing data come together, you get a very clear picture of the path of leads to revenue attributed to your final referral source.

Lead Source and Conversion Analysis

Quote #	Customer Name	Move Date	Estimated Amount	UTM Campaign	UTM Medium	UTM Source	Phone Data	Referral Source
49548	Jamie Brock	3/5/2025	$940.00	FortWorthGBP	organic	google	I found you online	Google
49547	Alyssa Kim	3/8/2025	$1,120.00	SanAntonioGBP	organic	google	my realtor told me about you	Referral
49549	Marcus Dean	3/10/2025	$980.00	DFW	PPC	Google	I found you online	Google paid ads
49550	Sierra Fields	3/12/2025	$750.00	DFW	PPC	Google	My friend Mary told me about you guys	Customer referral
49551	Ricky Torres	3/16/2025	$1,180.00		referral	Yelp	I found you on Google	Yelp
49552	Nina Caldwell	3/18/2025	$860.00		organic	direct	i google'd you	Google
49553	Logan Sharp	3/20/2025	$920.00			TruckQR	I think I saw you guys around	Saw Truck
49554	Daniela Cruz	3/22/2025	$1,030.00			Postcards	I Don't Remember	Postcards
49555	Harper Jones	3/26/2025	$890.00		organic	bing	found you online	Google/Bing

If you don't track exactly which marketing channels are driving profitable leads, you're gambling with your business. Unless you have unlimited money and don't care about profitability, you must know your precise lead attribution to reinvest wisely and grow.

Owner's Warning: Many marketing agencies will tell you that what I have just shared with you is not possible. **That's simply an ignorant lie.** Our clients have proven that it's 100% possible to obtain pinpoint-accurate data to make better decisions in their businesses.

Some agencies use excuses because this is a difficult process, requiring communication between you and your marketing agency. They must have intimate knowledge of how your CRM data connects to each lead. Most agencies are complacent, choosing the path of least resistance. Don't let their complacency distract you.

Owner's Hack: A major downside to using UTM parameters is that UTM data only sticks to the user for the first page visited on the website. If a user navigates to other pages on your website, UTMs will fall off ... UNLESS you use a special built code to fix this.

You can work with your marketing agency or developer to build a software code that forces the UTM data onto the users for the entire time they are on your website. But I would suggest using marketing-clarity.com instead.

Marketing Clarity has a code you can purchase and easily install on your website. The benefit to their code is that it forces the UTM data to stick to the user, going with them wherever they go on the website, without it getting lost on the next click.

It forces UTM data on the user from all the different channels that they come from, too: (Google organic, Yelp, Facebook, etc.). For example, if they come from Yelp, their code will automatically force correct UTM parameters onto the user. Even if they explore five different pages, when they submit a form, their UTM data is submitted to your CRM so that you can use it for better decisions and clarity in marketing ROI. If you don't use this code or fix, even if you use UTM data, you'll lose 90% of the valuable data from users visiting multiple pages—before they call in or fill out a quote form.

Lead Attribution Is Your Path to Profitable Marketing

This lead attribution process is your path to profitable, scalable marketing. It's your upper hand to beat your competitors in a competitive market. Every dollar you spend without knowing exactly where your leads come from is a dollar you're potentially throwing away. If you implement this lead attribution process, you will dominate your market while your competitors are left in the dust, asking themselves how you are growing so fast and blaming the economy for why their marketing "doesn't work."

You now have the roadmap: Integrate UTMs, capture the data in your CRM, and marry your marketing data with sales call information.

Welcome to presumptive business decision-making. Now you can stop making marketing decisions based on gut feelings and start making them based on real, cold, hard data.

The reality is that most of your competitors will never implement what you've just learned. I promise you. It's "too much work," and they will continue making emotional marketing decisions without insight. Their complacency is your business opportunity. When you know that your Google Business Profile generated $25,000 in revenue last month while your Google Ads lost money, you can double down on what works and cut what doesn't. That's how you scale profitably. The tools exist, the process is proven, and now you have no excuse not to implement it. It's time to execute while your competition stays lost in the dark.

Chapter Nine

THE AI WAVE

AI is the big buzz lately, and for a good reason. It's catching on exponentially faster than when Google first came to the market. In fact, ChatGPT achieved 365 billion annual searches in just two years—a milestone that took Google 11 years to reach.[2]

Such exponential growth proves that the AI wave is here to stay, suggesting a massive disruption. Your job, as an owner, is to figure out how you can leverage it for your continued success. Although Google is the focus of this book, AI is closely tied to Google search results, as the rise of users relying on AI to make decisions is increasing.

This isn't just theory; at Rotate Digital, we are experiencing it, implementing it, executing it, and getting results for our clients. Below is just a snippet of some recent results a client generated: 16 leads and 5 booked moves—from ChatGPT results alone in the last month! And we are only just beginning!

---

2   Et. "CHATGPT Crosses 365 Billion Annual Searches in 2024: Report." The Economic Times. Accessed September 4, 2025. https://economictimes. indiatimes.com/tech/artificial-intelligence/chatgpt-crosses-365-billion-annual-searches-in-2024-report/articleshow/121574978.cms.

186469249	Phone Call	Yes		chatgpt.com	(none)
186403026	Phone Call	Yes	4	chatgpt.com	(none)
186396284	Phone Call	Yes		chatgpt.com	(none)
186394669	Phone Call	Yes	6	chatgpt.com	(none)
184396535	Web Form			chatgpt.com	organic
182446291	Web Form			chatgpt.com	(none)
181789259	Web Form			chatgpt.com	(none)
181789097	Phone Call	No		chatgpt.com	(none)
180519890	Phone Call	No		chatgpt.com	organic
180516361	Web Form			chatgpt.com	organic
180422692	Web Form			chatgpt.com	(none)
180059897	Phone Call	Yes	7	chatgpt.com	organic
180053765	Web Form			chatgpt.com	organic
177631664	Web Form			chatgpt.com	organic
177547020	Phone Call	No		chatgpt.com	organic

Current Landscape

As of the writing of this book, Google is still dominating direct service search results; 87% of the US search market share (in May 2025) indicates people searching for local services.[3] And today, Google still offers the biggest leverage for your business marketing goals, but AI tools helping users make decisions are trending.

All this to say, Google is still dominant. So, let's not panic about needing to transform our online marketing right now to be geared

---

3   Rijo, Luis. "Google's Search Dominance Continues, Capturing 87% Market Share in Q1 2025." PPC Land, April 27, 2025. https://ppc.land/googles-search-dominance-continues-capturing-87-market-share-in-q1-2025/.

toward AI results. You can make wise decisions to be ahead of the game.

How ChatGPT and Other AI Platforms Rank

Changes are happening in the way people are searching with AI. Instead of users googling "movers las vegas," they are using AI and entering, "what's the best moving company in las vegas?" or "what's the cheapest way to move in las vegas?" We're witnessing a transition from keyword queries to conversational questions, which affects how content is discovered and consumed:

- Traditional search: "Moving company Dallas."
- AI-era search: "What does a move from Dallas to Austin cost for a 4 bedroom house?"

AI platforms prefer structured, trust-based content (something you already created if you followed the process in Chapter 4 on Google Organic SERBM results). If you want your moving company to be visible across AI platforms, your brand needs to clearly communicate:

- **Who you are** – Your business identity and brand.
- **Your services** – Clear service descriptions.
- **Where you offer services** – Geographic service areas.

Your information must be consistent across all platforms where your business appears online, so make sure that you provide comprehensive answers to these questions. One of the ways to do this is through schema markups.

Schema Markup

Schema markup is the language that helps search engines and AI understand your content structure. It's essential for:

- Service-specific pages
- FAQ sections
- Business information
- Reviews and ratings

Any page you want crawled over by AI and ranked needs schema. If you're working with an SEO company, ensure that they're implementing schema markup, particularly on FAQ and service pages.

Trusted Directory Listings

AI platforms source information from established, trusted directories. Essential listings for movers include:

- Google Maps
- Apple Maps
- Bing Places
- Facebook
- Instagram
- Yelp
- Angi's List
- Better Business Bureau
- Thumbtack
- Local industry-specific directories

Each listing should maintain consistent NAP (name, address, phone) information and service descriptions. If you don't have these listings with your business information, take the time to set them up sooner rather than later.

Now, if you're reading this and thinking, *Man, this looks similar to the stuff you need for traditional SEO,* you are spot on. You can't ride the AI wave without implementing foundational SEO first.

It's Actually Working

Current data shows that while AI traffic volume is less than Google's, AI conversion rates are high and growing. Users trust what AI is spitting out! When leads do click through to sites from AI platforms, they're highly qualified and convert at exceptional rates (conversion meaning click to booked job). Here are three snapshots of clients' monthly AI results, which support everything we've been talking about:

- **Client 1:** 16 sessions from ChatGPT resulted in 5 conversions (31% conversion rate).
- **Client 2:** 5 sessions resulted in 3 conversions (60% conversion rate).
- **Client 3:** 60 sessions resulted in 33 conversions (55% conversion rate).

This high conversion rate occurs because AI provides a better search experience with higher user trust. Users get comprehensive answers and arrive at your website already informed and ready to take action.

Owner's Warning: Before AI, you would write valuable content, the blog would receive lots of impressions, and generate a ton of clicks. Now, with AI, "The Click Paradox" occurs, meaning you will create blogs that generate tons of impressions, but you'll have no clicks. This is due to the blog ranking well. It appears in AI-generated answers and receives high impressions, but fewer clicks because the searcher's question is answered immediately. Don't worry about this. If AI is picking up your content, it's a good sign of valuable rankings ahead!

Do not use specific AI platforms to optimize; focus on doing standard foundational work. Since we don't know which AI model will experience massive growth or adoption, or what new models will come out, don't spend too much effort focusing on one model. No matter the model, the foundation will work.

Secret Sauce: How to Win in AI Results

Step 1: Claim and Verify Major Profiles

Ensure your business is properly listed and verified on:

- Google Maps
- Apple Maps
- Bing Places
- Facebook
- Instagram
- Yelp
- Angi's List
- Better Business Bureau
- Thumbtack

Step 2: Implement Clear FAQs

Create comprehensive FAQ sections that are:

- **Unique to your business** – Address specific questions your customers are asking.
- **Locally relevant** – Include area-specific concerns and regulations.
- **Service-specific** – Cover industry-specific questions.

Track questions that come through your sales and customer service teams to identify gaps in your FAQ content.

Step 3: Focus on Foundational SEO

Work with an SEO company that emphasizes:

- Holistic, long-term strategies over shortcuts.
- Proper schema markup implementation.
- Local citation building.
- Review generation and management.
- Page speed optimization.

Avoid agencies promising quick rankings through shortcuts, as these often result in long-term penalties.

Step 4: Don't Be a One-Trick, Content-Writing Pony

Write valuable content, but don't stop there. You need to expand your content presence beyond blogs on your website, with:

- **YouTube:** Google emphasized YouTube heavily at its recent I/O conference.
- **Instagram:** Google is now indexing professional profiles (as of July 15th, 2025).
- **Facebook:** Maintain an active, informative business presence.

Step 5: Write *Valuable* Content

Whether content is created by humans or AI doesn't matter to search engines. What matters is:

- Value to the end user.
- Comprehensive answers to user questions.
- Unique expertise and experience.
- Natural, helpful flow.

Follow the suggestions in Chapter 4 on how to write valuable content on your website.

Step 6: Monitor AI Traffic and Conversions

Install proper lead attribution (as discussed in the previous chapter) to determine which conversions are coming from Google and which are coming from AI searches.

Don't accept your marketing team saying, "We can't track that." Demand clear data on your lead sources. Going forward, you should know exactly where every lead originated from and be able to make data-driven decisions about your marketing investments.

Bottom Line

The way to win on AI is to win on Google. Currently, AI platforms source their information from the internet, which primarily means Google's indexed results. When you excel in Google SEO rankings, you'll automatically improve your visibility across AI platforms. We've covered reviews, schema markup, URL structure, and using solid local backlinks as standard places to start; you'll be happily surprised that when you address these areas, AI leads will flow in.

> Remember, it's not about being the first to AI, it's about not being the last.

I'll leave you with some of the most frequently asked questions we receive about AI to help guide you in your AI implementation.

If you've eaten up the information in this chapter and want more, Rotate Digital filmed an hour-long webinar on AI, expanding on the details. Check it out here: www.rotatedigital.com/book-ai-webinar.

FAQs Around AI

Q: How can I set up UTMs for ChatGPT traffic?

A: You cannot directly set up UTMs for ChatGPT. AI platforms pull URLs from existing web sources: your Google Business Profile, website, social media profiles, etc. The UTM tracking comes from these source URLs. To properly view ChatGPT traffic, you need advanced tracking systems that can identify the referral source and attribute it correctly. Use marketingclarity.com and buy their "Sticky UTM" product to install on your website, and you'll be able to track leads that come from AI!

Q: How long does it take for ChatGPT to see new information?

A: The timeline varies depending on the AI model being used. Older models use older trained data, while newer models access more current information. Many AI platforms now use "retrieval augmented generation" (RAG), which pulls real-time information and fact-checks it. While there's no documented timeline, like "seven days for indexing," newer AI models generally provide more current data.

Q: Should I implement schema markup on every page?

A: Include schema markup on pages where you want to drive traffic—primarily service-specific pages and service area pages—and in content that answers customer questions. Use schema with your blogs if the content contains purchase intent or valuable information that could lead to conversions. Schema markups cost money to build and develop, so focus on the higher-priority pages first.

Q: What about content generated by AI?

A: Again, the generation method doesn't matter. What matters is the quality and value of the content to users. Google has explicitly stated that it doesn't care if content is AI-generated, as long as it's valuable. Focus on creating content that:

- Answers questions with unique expertise.
- Draws from your business experience.
- Provides genuine value to readers.
- Flows naturally and helpfully.

Use the content ideas we addressed in the SERBM/blog chapter as inspiration and have confidence in your value. We have seen hundreds of our clients' blogs and content rank in top spots on Google, and they were mainly generated from AI to create value for the user.

Q: How can I acquire backlinks organically?

A: Organic backlink acquisition strategies include:

- Local citation directories.
- Partnership opportunities with complementary local businesses.
- Creating valuable content that naturally attracts links.
- Community involvement and local business networking.

Important Caveat: Don't simply exchange random links with other businesses. Ensure any backlink opportunity provides genuine value and flows naturally within relevant content.

Q: What's the most important takeaway for local service businesses?

A: Don't abandon Google SEO for AI optimization. Google is still the primary driver of revenue for local service businesses. AI platforms have high conversion rates, but success comes from implementing foundational SEO practices that benefit both traditional rankings and AI rankings.

Chapter Ten

CLAIM YOUR DIGITAL EMPIRE

Back in 1901, a drilling crew led by Anthony Lucas was on the verge of giving up on a small hill called Spindletop near Beaumont, Texas. They'd been drilling for months, hitting nothing but dry holes that broke their equipment. Most people said there was no oil in Texas, that the real oil was up north in Pennsylvania.

On January 10, 1901, at 1,020 feet deep, the drill bit hit something different. Suddenly, mud bubbled up. Next came natural gas. And then … BOOM! A geyser of black crude shot 150 feet into the air, producing more oil in one day than the rest of the world combined.

The difference between Lucas and all the guys who gave up? He understood that oil drilling wasn't about luck; it was about strategy, persistence, and drilling in the right spots with the right methods. This is you today. Drilling for digital oil, for a flow of consistent leads that can change the trajectory of your business, your life, the lives of your employees, and even your family, for generations to come.

We've covered a ton of ground here, from understanding that Google is your digital real estate empire to building your website that actually sells, from dominating Google Maps to running profitable ad campaigns that don't burn your money. We've discussed the future of AI, the critical importance of lead attribution, and how to hold agencies accountable for real results.

> You can now take control of your business, your lead flow, and your digital assets.

No more wondering where your next customer is coming from. No more getting jerked around by agencies that can't explain where your monthly spend is going. No more watching your competitors dominate your areas online while you're stuck playing defense and catch-up.

But here's what I really want you to walk away with: This isn't just about marketing.

This is about building the moving company you always envisioned. The one that doesn't rely on word-of-mouth alone or pray that the phone rings. The one that can scale on your timeline, compete with the big boys, and actually put more cash in your pocket instead of throwing it at marketing black holes.

I get it. Learning about all this information and what to do may feel overwhelming. You didn't start your moving company to become a Google expert or decode marketing agency B.S. You started it to help families move their lives, build something of your own, and maybe create generational wealth along the way.

Here's the brutal truth: Your competition isn't waiting for you to figure this out. While you're debating whether to invest in professional photography or wondering if you really need multiple Google

Business Profiles, your competitors are claiming digital real estate in your market today, right now. They're showing up on Google when your potential customers search for movers. They're building trust through reviews and rankings. They're scaling their moving businesses while you sit on the fence.

> Here's the flip side—and this is what gets me fired up for you: Most moving companies are doing this stuff completely wrong.

They're using stock photos of people who appear to have never lifted a box in their lives. They're building websites that seem like they were designed in 2005. They're throwing money at Google Ads without any clue what their actual ROI is. They're missing calls, not following up with texts, and handing customers over to their competitors, one lead at a time. This is your opportunity. This is your chance to dominate this dog-eat-dog digital world.

When you implement what we've covered in this book: the real photography, the sales-focused website, the multiple map locations, the proper lead attribution, and the smart advertising strategies, you're not just improving your marketing. You're building a more valuable business to one day sell or pass on to family members for generations.

You're creating predictable lead flow instead of crossing your fingers and hoping. You're building systems that work whether you're in the office or taking a week off on vacation with your kids in Disney World. You're compounding and developing the assets in this book over time. It's the snowball effect, starting small and growing until it's rolling down that hill, getting bigger and bigger every year.

You don't have to do everything at once. Hell, you probably shouldn't try to. But you do need to start somewhere, and you need to start now.

Maybe it's hiring a photographer this month to get rid of those embarrassing stock photos. Maybe it's setting up proper lead attribution so you finally know what's working and what's not for your marketing channels. Maybe it's opening that second Google Business Profile location we talked about.

Maybe, just maybe, it's breaking up with your marketing agency that has turned your monthly retainer into their own passive income, all while your ROI flatlines and you're left asking yourself, *What's actually working?*

Now you can own digital marketing success. Pick one proven tactic in this book that resonates the most with you and execute on it. Get it done and done right. Then move to the next. Step by step, you can rise above your competition.

And remember, this isn't about becoming perfect overnight. It's about becoming better than your competitors, one step at a time. Most of them are managing their marketing so poorly that even getting halfway good at these marketing strategies will put you miles ahead of them.

I wasn't exaggerating when I talked about generational wealth earlier. The moving industry is going through a massive shift. The companies that dial in their digital marketing will dominate the next decade. The ones that don't will become irrelevant, and as we have seen recently, start to close their doors.

I've watched $2 million moving companies become $8 million companies by properly implementing these strategies. I've seen anxiety-ridden owners go from stress-eating, nail-biting, and panicking about shutting down to confidently planning expansions into new markets and positioning themselves for acquisitions. On the flip side, I've also seen companies stick their heads in the sand, ignore the digital revolution, and slowly watch their market share disappear (to competitors who were willing to adapt), ultimately closing up shop or selling their businesses for pennies on the dollar.

Don't be them.

I could have written a 500-page manual filled with technical jargon and complicated theories. Instead, I gave you the real strategies that actually move the needle, explained in a way that makes sense for busy business owners who have better things to do than become marketing experts.

Take action and use this book. Don't let it collect dust. Your business needs this today. And when you start seeing results, when your phone starts ringing more, when your competition starts wondering what in the world you're doing differently, when your business starts growing faster than you thought possible, remember that it all started with deciding to take control of your digital presence.

Your digital real estate empire awaits. Google is the land. Your website and Google Business Profile aren't just marketing tools; they're your assets to produce tens of thousands of dollars-plus every month in cash flow. Now get out there and claim what's yours.

It's time to build that empire!

P.S. If you need help implementing any of these strategies, you know where to find us: www.rotatedigital.com. But honestly, even if you never work with our agency, I'll sleep better at night knowing that if you use what I've taught you, you'll be one of a handful of moving company owners not getting screwed over by mediocre marketing agencies.

HOW TO SEPARATE GREAT MARKETING COMPANIES FROM B.S. MARKETING COMPANIES

I included this bonus chapter because business owners constantly ask me: "How do I know if a marketing company is legit or just selling lies?" They all sound the same, but only a few are actually great.

I see too many owners who don't know how to interview marketing companies. They can't see through their lies, challenge the details of their work, or hold them accountable. The unfortunate result? Owners get screwed out of money, get fed more fog, and it delays their ability to get the results they're ultimately looking for.

In this chapter, I will share with you our foundational metric-driven dashboard to help you measure and track your marketing campaigns to ensure they are performing as needed in the right timeframe. I've also given you a list of challenging questions designed to gauge how agencies respond. This allows you to assess how vague or specific their answers are, giving you more or less confidence in them. These questions are meant to be tough, and you can use them to build a great partnership with your marketing agency by establishing real transparency, real metrics, real results, and real expectations from day one. To find the answers you need, go to the link at the bottom of these questions. I'm not providing them to you in the book because I don't want other agencies to swipe them and use the answers to pretend they know what they're doing.

Your Core and Critical KPI Dashboard for Measuring SEO Success

It's extremely important to measure the results of your SEO process. I find many owners struggle to measure results, and very few have clarity in what leading critical KPIs to use to have confidence in the direction of their marketing campaign.

These core KPIs, critical KPIs, and Your Most Important Number (MIN) are your guiding metrics to measure your marketing efforts. I've swiped this concept from my business mentor, Lee Benson, in his book *Your Most Important Number*, and applied it to your SEO efforts (I highly recommend reading his book).

Owner's Note: As your marketing company, we are your vendor and partner in the success of your business. Our sole job is to help move you closer to valuable visibility and more sales to create an ROI for your investment. These KPIs are primarily focused on measuring your first year with a marketing company. After year one, or at any time, these metrics can change based on your unique business needs.

Core KPIs for SEO (month 1-4):

1. Increasing GBP keyword relevancy and volume.

In your Google Business Profile performance stats is a breakdown of keywords driving impressions and clicks to your GBP. In the first 3-5 months, you will want to see your keywords becoming more relevant to your brand. These sales-relevant keywords need to start shifting to show an increasing amount of searches, month-over-month. For example, if the keyword "moving company" is not on the list, in the first 3-5 months, you'll want to see that appear in the top 10 list. If it was already there, the search volume of that keyword should be increasing.

2. Increasing SERBM (SERP) results; avg. traffic.

In this beginning time period, you want to see average traffic volume to your website increasing; this is a good sign that your campaign is trending in the right direction. You can use any tool to track this. We use Ahrefs.com—this tool allows you to gain intimate insight into keywords driving traffic to your website. Eventually, you'll want to make sure that your sales-relevant keywords, like "moving company" or "movers [insert city]," increase in ranking and search volume.

3. Increasing GBP calls.

This is a metric within your GBP performance dashboard. You will want to see an increase in calls from your GBP. It's not a perfect measurement, but it's a leading KPI in your Google Business Profile, potentially pointing to increased map visibility.

4. Increasing map visibility.

In the first four months, you want your visibility to move into the top 1-3 placements on the map results. Your agency should be showing you these results. If not, you can see it for yourself, using a tool like leadsnap.com

Critical KPIs for SEO (month 4-9)

As your timeline continues, you'll begin to place a heavier focus on these critical KPIs. These KPIs are more geared toward outcome data. Your focus now is not primarily on your core metrics (although you won't stop looking at these). You'll bring your attention to the following outcome metrics.

1. **Leads in your CRM from Google**: At this point, you want to still see increasing leads coming from Google into your CRM. When they are growing in volume compared to your previous period or previous year, that is your sweet spot.

2. **Calls from Google:** Calls from Google should be increasing. You can track this with a call tracking software or from what your sales team inputs into your CRM.

3. **Organic traffic from sales-relevant keywords:** Now, you can hyper-focus on sales-relevant keywords to determine if traffic is increasing to your website from these keywords.

Your Most Important Number (MIN) (approaching month 12)

Your most important number is your Google sales.

As you approach the end of the first year, if not sooner, your MIN needs to indicate that you're closing more jobs from Google. Your goal is to see a positive ROI from your investment. Two calculations will help you paint the story of your marketing campaigns and ROI.

Method 1 is a snapshot of a specific month or quarter that you can look at to determine your Google sales and what you spent to get them. If this number is positive, it means your campaign will potentially continue to pay out and that the current snapshot is winning for your business. It helps you justify with confidence if you can continue your spend on your marketing efforts.

Let's say that one month you had $55,000 in sales from Google. Then you compare that to the previous year, and see that last year it was $35,000 in sales from Google. That's an additional $20,000 in sales from Google. Now, let's say you spend $4,000 a month on SEO for this specific month: You are getting a 4X ROI

Method 2 is a look at your longer period of investment, through month 12. Add up all your Google revenue over the last year and compare it to the previous year to see if you have a positive ROI.

For example, you would look back over a year and note that you had $522,000 in sales from Google. Compare that to the previous year, when you only had $352,000 in sales. That's an increase of $170,000 in additional sales. If you were investing $5,000 per month for 12 months, you would have a 2.8X ROI on your yearly investment.

You want to use both methods to get a more comprehensive picture of what's happening with your spend. If you've been investing in SEO for one year, for example, and use Method 1 to measure month 12 (your current month), you might see a 4X ROI, whereas if you use Method 2 and assess the *entire year*, you may see only a 2.8X ROI. Maybe you even see these numbers flipped. The goal is to use both of these methods to calculate your ROI for the entire year to see what it's produced—along with calculating a snapshot of your current month (or your most recent quarter) to see where your ROI is heading. Don't depend on one method over another. Use both to figure out where you're going and where you have been.

In Method 1, your snapshot showed a healthier ROI. In Method 2, your yearly investment returned a below-average ROI (shoot for your first major KPI milestone to be a 3X return and grow it from there). You can use these methods to make a confident data-driven decision for your business and marketing efforts.

For this specific example, I would continue the SEO process while calculating the monthly snapshot ROI to monitor month-to-month progress and make sure your ROI trend continues in the right direction. Since I know that SEO results can take time to build up momentum, the 2.8X ROI for the year doesn't cause me to cancel the process altogether, as Method 1 is showing positive trending ROI. Use both these calculations to discuss your concerns with your marketing company. An aggregated 12 months of a below-average ROI doesn't mean good results are not coming to you. You can let the SEO process play out to see if your 4X ROI monthly snapshot continues. Or you can move to another agency so they can continue building on this positive momentum, giving you more confidence.

> The goal of providing these KPIs is to help you make objective, data-driven business decisions instead of emotional ones.

I've seen owners make emotional decisions despite the positive ROI data, ultimately destroying their long-term investment. If you use this foundational KPI dashboard to measure your success, your objective decision-making will help you get the outcomes you need for your business. Don't burn down the building you just built with your hard-earned money by making a rash, emotional, data-less, and subjective decision.

Questions and Insights to Demand from Your Agency

I wanted to give you a list of questions to ask your marketing agency to help you cut through the fog and B.S. Everyone will mention backlinks, but can they share their specific backlink strategy, explain the value of different types of backlinks, or outline their quality standards? Or can they explain their PPC strategy and how they will leverage offline conversions to help you get better leads? The biggest thing you're looking for is whether the agency or their salesperson can talk specifically and level-headedly about their plan, expected results, and SEO approach. Often, I see owners not knowing the right questions to ask. The answers to these questions contain explanations about why each insight matters and what you need to be aware of. Take this list and start using it as a *tactical* tool to hold your marketing company or marketing person accountable for the results you need them to generate.

Questions for Your Marketing Agency

Measuring Success for SEO:

1. What core KPIs measure a successful SEO spend?
2. What critical KPIs measure a successful SEO spend?
3. What is your most important number used to track success in my SEO campaign?
4. How do you measure success in SEO and marketing?

I've given you the answers to these questions at the start of this chapter, but see how your marketing agency responds and how their answers align with your business goals.

ROI:

1. How do you specifically tie ROI to SEO and other marketing investments?
2. How do you measure the baseline of my prior Google revenue?
3. Will you be able to show me the exact lead attribution for each marketing channel?
4. Are ROI and results purely based on the money I am spending with your company?
5. What do you define as conversions?

PPC:

1. Will you track conversions of my PPC and SEO separately?
2. Do you separate PPC branded bids versus non-branded bids?
3. What PPC strategy specific to clicks and conversions is being implemented?
4. Do you upload offline conversions to Google?
5. Do you leverage landing pages for PPC to optimize conversions?
6. Are there standard website conversion rates for your top-performing clients? If so, can you show me?

SEO:

1. What keywords are we focusing on to improve their rankings?

2. Do you specifically focus on Map Pack rankings in the SEO process?

3. What mile radius does my Google Business Profile have the potential to reach?

4. How possible is it for me to 100% dominate the top three spots on the Map Pack?

Backlinks:

1. What kind of backlinks are used in the SEO strategy, and when do they get used?

2. What are the quality standards of backlinks you acquire for my company?

3. How do you generate different types of backlinks?

4. Do you purchase guest posts? If so, what are the standards, e.g., traffic volume, country of origin, how recent the traffic is to the website?

Content:

1. What is the purpose of blogs?

2. How do I know if blogging is working for my SEO strategy?

3. Do you leverage AI to create content? Why or why not? What kind of human involvement is used in content creation?

AI:

1. How do you optimize and leverage my brand for AI searches?

2. What AI LLM (learning language model) is the most valuable today, and are you optimizing a specific AI?

3. What specific deliverables apply to my AI ranking?

4. Do you have clients getting conversions from AI? Can you show me some examples?

Other:

1. What are the hard deliverables I can expect to get in this SEO process?

2. Do I own my website after it's built?

3. How do I increase my SEO rankings faster?

4. What percentage of your clients are winning? How do you determine this answer? (This is my favorite question, because 99% of agencies don't specifically track which clients are winning or losing.)

5. What are some examples of clients that didn't get good results with your company, and why? What do I need to do to give my company the best chance at succeeding?

6. What do I get on monthly calls?

There is absolutely no excuse for you as an owner to write off SEO and PPC as a way to grow your business. You may have had bad SEO and PPC results because of your business model or sales process, but it could be that you just need to work with a better marketing agency to partner with you and get the results you've been dreaming of. The best moving companies use SEO to grow their business, and if you write off SEO and PPC altogether, you will always be a company that struggles to hit new milestones. Guaranteed.

All the insights and answers to these questions can be found at https://www.rotatedigital.com/bonus-answers or by using the QR code here.

ACKNOWLEDGMENTS

I want to thank the many people who made this book possible.

To my wife, who believed in me when I started this agency right at the birth of our second child, with little money and everything to lose. Your faith changed everything. Meg, you are the best mother and wife, and a gift from God to me and our family. While I was head-down writing chapters, you managed our home and cared for not only our kids but an amazing foster baby. Through all the spit-ups, chaos, and long days, I hope this book proves that it was all worth it. Thank you for giving me the opportunity to write this book and supporting me in this 10-year chapter of our life. I love you.

To Ashley and Mike, thank you for your strategic handling of the Amazon and design chaos with a crazy timeline. I'm beyond grateful.

To Hilary, because behind every CEO with big ideas and tactical knowledge is a brilliant editor who makes them slow down, think clearer, and actually cross the finish line.

To our clients, who trusted us with their hard-earned money, allowing us the opportunity to help your company become the moving titan in your market, this book exists because of what we've learned together.

To my team, for giving me the encouragement and time to write this book while you kept everything running smoothly. You supported me through every chapter. Thank you for sharing all your knowledge and incredible skill sets. Because of your expertise, this book will bring life-changing results to business owners everywhere. I am deeply grateful.

And to every moving company owner grinding it out every day, building their business and creating something life-changing—this book is for you. You're the reason we do what we do.

ABOUT THE AUTHOR

Travis Weathers is first a husband to one beautiful wife, Meg, and dad of three amazing kids (currently with a fourth kid, a blessed foster baby). He is the founder and CEO of Rotate Digital, started in 2019, which rose to become the largest #1 marketing agency for moving companies. Rotate Digital has worked with over 300 moving companies, been recognized as one of the 5000 fastest-growing private companies on Inc. 5000 multiple years in a row, and hit the top 100 fastest-growing marketing agencies in the nation.

Travis and his team at Rotate Digital work with the largest privately owned moving companies in the nation to help them dominate Google and maximize their ROI with SEO and PPC. He speaks at multiple industry conferences and is a straight talker who values results over fluff. Travis wrote this no B.S. guide to give moving company owners the clarity and tools they need to beat their competitors and grow with profit.

MOVERS MARKETING: *A No B.S. Guide for Moving Companies to Win on Google and Maximize ROI* is his first book. It isn't theory. It's all about the exact system and tactical implementation Rotate Digital uses to dominate competitors and profit from Google—without getting lost in the noise of empty marketing promises.

DISCLAIMER

The information provided within this book is for general informational, educational, and entertainment purposes only. The author and publisher are not offering such information as business, investment, or legal advice, or any other kind of professional advice, and the advice and ideas contained herein may not be suitable for your situation.

Any use of the information provided within this book is at your own risk, and it is provided without any express or implied warranties or guarantees on the part of the author or publisher. No warranty may be created or extended by sales representatives or written sales materials. You should seek the services of a competent professional before beginning any business endeavor or investment.

Neither the author nor the publisher shall be held liable or responsible to any person or entity with respect to any financial, commercial, or other loss or damages (including but not limited to special, incidental, or consequential damages) caused or alleged to have been caused, directly or indirectly, by the use of any of the information contained herein.

9 798234 009357